A GLIMPSE OF ASSAM

A GLIMPSE OF ASSAM

SUSAN R. WARD

Published by

FacsiMile Publisher
12 Pragati Market
Ashok Vihar, Ph-2
Delhi - 110052, India
Phone: 011-47034999
Email: www.facsimilepublishers.com
info@facsimilepublishers.com

Distribution Network
gyanbooks.com
India, USA, Canada, UK, Australia

ISBN: 978-93-6896-250-2 (PB)
First Published, 1885

2nd Impression 2025

Printed at: Gyan Press, Delhi.

A GLIMPSE OF ASSAM
Author: SUSAN R. WARD

A GLIMPSE OF ASSAM.

EDITED & PUBLISHED

BY MRS. S. R. WARD.

CALCUTTA:
PRINTED BY THOMAS S. SMITH, CITY PRESS,
12, BENTINCK STREET.

1884.

CONTENTS.

PREFACE.

THERE may be some who think *Assam* a most uninteresting subject about which to write a book; there are others who have been long in the province who say, "we know enough already of Assam," but we believe there are a far greater number who have sufficient interest in the future welfare of the country, to welcome an effort to bring its natural charms and grand resources into notice, and by this means promote its general prosperity.

There are also many who know almost nothing of a country so far outside the usual route of travel, and who desire information which is not easily obtained, as there is a decided lack of books on the subject. "Robinson's Assam," published more than two score years ago, has long been out of print; Dr. Hunter's "Statistics of Assam," though a valuable book for reference, is large, expensive, and too statistical for general reading.

We fancy, too, there are many at a distance who have a financial interest in the great Tea industry of the province, and others who have kindred or friends engaged in it, who would feel a warm interest even in only a "Glimpse" of the surroundings.

If this brief descriptive glimpse of the chief points of interest in the country meets a want which will tend to the welfare of the people for whose best interest the writer has devoted many years of the prime of life, we are content.

We ask the indulgence of our readers to any inaccuracies they may meet, as our sources of information have nearly been confined to the two books above mentioned and personal observation from a long residence in the country.

We are also greatly indebted to one of the oldest residents, and best informed in regard to Assam,—Dr. C. J. Simons, for a careful review of the manuscript, and information and suggestions of value in the preparation.

S. R. Ward.

OPENING GLIMPSE.

CHAPTER I.

A TRAVELLER, when nearing the province of Assam, thus enthusiastically expresses himself: "We are now approaching the classic soil of India: scenes where ancient gods disported themselves with goddesses to the infinite spiritual edification of gaping crowds of mortals. It was here in Kamrupa that Shiva married Parboti the daughter of Himalaya, and during the marriage procession danced * * before his bride. And higher up in Assam the same Shiva went about in the guise of a mendicant, corrupting matrons and maids to the great pain of his young wife. These things are mentioned *honorably* in the two great epic poems of India." This quotation gives a glimpse of the sensual character of the Hindu religion and, as a natural consequence, a glimpse of the character of its votaries. "Like priest, like people." Hinduism without doubt greatly flourished in Assam in former times, there are several noted places of pilgrimage, and hill tops in every part of the province are crowned with temples that now tell of decaying Hinduism ; no effort is made to repair these massive and costly structures, and many are hidden in rank vegetation. The present generation has not seen a new temple built. Over dark Assam

> The morning light is breaking,
> The darkness disappears.

The province of Assam, which is the most north-east limit of British India, has attracted little attention from the outside world, and been little known till within the past half century. The discovery of indigenous tea, and the rapid growth of that industry, has awakened a growing interest in the rich fertile valley of the Brahmaputra. When the British took possession in 1827, the country had been distracted by internal feuds, devastated and partly depopulated by wars with neighbouring tribes ; the new regimé speedily changed this state of anarchy to one of continued peace and prosperity, such as had not been known in the province for generations.

The name Assam, originated with a former conquering race, the Ahoms, and is said to signify peerless or unequalled. Assam, in some respects, will not bear comparison with some of the more settled and civilized portions of India, but the fertility of the soil, the salubrity of the climate, the number of rivers and streams, and in grandeur of hill scenery, we venture to say, Assam has scarcely a rival in any part of India of equal extent.

It has been facetiously termed "the happy valley," "the last end of creation," "the jumping off place;" the latter may seem applicable from the fact that the regions around,—north, east, and south—Bhutan, Chinese Tartary, the Shan country, and the north of Burmah, are virtually unknown regions.

Assam is usually approached through India's great metropolis, Calcutta. From Sealdah station a train brings you to Goalundo, a distance of 150 miles. At this point you meet a steamer that started from Calcutta a week previous, and winding through the delta of the Ganges, called the Sunderbunds, stops for passengers at this railway terminus; there you can embark in very comfortable double-decked steamers for any part of Assam, and be provided with a cabin and a liberal table. If time is valuable you can reach Dubri, the first station in Assam, by taking a train from Calcutta to Sara, and by different stages of train and boat cross the country to Dubri in about twenty-five hours, which the steamer will be four or five days in reaching from Goalundo. On the map you will find Dubri just at the point where the Brahmaputra turns north-east, from this point the valley of Assam lies on each side the river, following a north-easterly course for about 800 miles, terminating above Sadiya, where the river again bends directly north to the Himalayas.

This noble river, one of the largest in the world, son of Brahma, as its name signifies, is the great artery of Assam, veins from the north and south flow into it and form channels of communication with the interior. Thirty-four tributaries flow from the northern and twenty-four from the southern mountains; in respect to being well watered, Assam is probably *unequalled.*

On leaving Dubri, a few hours steaming brings you to Goalpara, a picturesque place with its lofty wooded hill dotted here and there with a bungalow. A climb to the top is well rewarded with an extensive view of the country for many miles, and of the grand Bhutan and Himalaya ranges on the north and the Garrow hills on the south.

Another day's steaming (at night the steamers always lie anchored) and you reach Goahati, the prettiest station on the river side, the bank being protected from the encroachment of the ever shifting river current, by the rocky spurs of the Khassia range jutting out into the stream. The station, in bygone days, was the seat of native royalty, the largest town in the province, and for some years after British possession, was the residence of the highest officials, but since the heads of the Governmental Department moved to Shillong, European residents are few, though the native town is a large and busy one.

The next station above is Tezpore, on the north bank; from the river you see but little of the station except the bungalows on the hill tops along the bank. From this point up to Debrughur, the terminal steamer station, there are no stations or even villages directly on the river. On each side a monotonous low level bank covered with grass jungle, meets the eye, and occasionally a dark blue hill in the distance; but there is no sign of life except flocks of water birds, or wild buffaloes coming to drink, or alligators sunning themselves on the sand. It will not be strange if you weary of the slow progress, and the monotony of the trip. The lifeless scene is due mainly to the river which, instead of being called a son of Brahma (the Creator), more properly might be termed, the son of Shiva (the Destroyer); for destruction is its constant work, breaking away embankments and piling up sand bars that obstruct navigation. The rapid current quickly changes its course, and this makes it necessary for the steamers to employ a pilot, changing them at frequent stages, and also to anchor at sundown. Even with these precautions they are often detained for hours, and sometimes days on a sand bar. In the cool season a dense fog settles over the river, and obliterates the course of the channel, till it lifts, frequently as late as ten or eleven o'clock, before the steamer can proceed.

The shifting current accounts for the absence of human habitation on the banks. Villages that were miles inland and had stood for years, are gradually encroached upon, and as you pass you can see the gardens of plantain trees and betel-nut, tumbling into the swift current. Still, what would the province be without this great glorious river? No wonder the superstitious inhabitants believe it flows directly from the feet of a god, and so pure and sacred is it, that it will wash their sins away, or at death, bear them to heaven on its bosom.

In the light of truth it is indeed the gift of God and a fountain of blessing to the people; its pure air has been the means of restoring to health many a fever-stricken invaild. Our traveller, we will suppose, is not in search of health, but has his eyes wide open to discover the beauties of this magnificent valley. After leaving Tezpore the steamer drops anchor at places with a *name*, but scarcely a habitation, they are mostly *mukhs*, that is, *mouths* of some stream communicating with stations or Tea estates in the interior; you reach Dhunseri-

STEAMER TO CARRY PASSENGERS
AND FREIGHT FROM ASSAM TO CALCUTTA.

mukh, Kukila-mukh, Jhansi-mukh, Dikho-mukh, &c. At the end of twelve or fourteen days, which a "*stick on the sand,*" or, a break of machinery may prolong to twenty, you gladly reach the end of the steamer route, Debrughur,—formerly on the river bank, now by the capricous river, five miles distant in the cold season. In the rainy season the river is navigable to Sadiya, sixty-two miles north. Any one observing the amount of cargo the river steamers bring and take away, will form some idea of the country's great industry. Tea manufacture,—chiefly carried on by foreigners,—supports two lines of steamers running weekly from Calcutta to Assam.

A traveller arriving about the middle of October, when the rainy season is over, can enjoy about five months of the most healthy season of the year for travel, and in a climate as delightful as is to be found in the world, dry, cool and unchangeable; there is no need of an umbrella or any of the requisites of bad weather. A morning fog may be thought a drawback to comfort, but it is not considered unhealthy; it is rather to be enjoyed as Infinite Wisdom's compensation for the absence of rain, keeping all nature fresh and verdant.

At this season the traveller can with comfort make a tour of the province riding, driving, or by elephant. The air is comparatively free from malarious influences and the roads, unless off the main routes, have become passable; where other means of conveyance is impracticable an elephant is *a sine qua non.* Much has been done to improve the means of communication between the stations and tea estates, still in a country where rivers and streams are so numerous and the annual rainfall an average of 100 inches, much yet remains to be done in the elevation of roads and in bridging rivers and ditches to make travelling safe and comfortable. However, braving some hardships on this score, a most enjoyable tour may be made through wild virgin forests, richly decked with ferns and flowers, now and then broken by the low level rice fields of the villagers whose thatched roofs are seen among the trees on its outer edge, and here and there a tea plantation with its bungalow, tea-house, and cooly lines, and all around rows of the dark green fragrant bush stretch away over plain, slope or hill.

On any high ground, looking northward, when the air is clear, an enchanting view may be seen of the snow-capped pinnacles of the Himalayas. This grand glorious scene rivets one's gaze to the spot; the glistening snow, covering successive undulations of valley and height, are so clearly distinct, that we can scarcely believe they are at a great distance.

CLIMATE AND LANGUAGE.

CHAPTER II.

MUCH has been said, and too much believed, about the unhealthiness of the country. On new clearances and in some localities, there is more or less danger of fever from malaria; the same is true in other countries, but in an open and cleared situation with proper care, the best of health can be enjoyed in this much maligned Assam.

Some new-comers, ignorant or careless of the consequences, expose themselves unnecessarily to the hot sun of midday or to be drenched in rain, and what is especially obnoxious to health, travel through the jungle in the rainy reason; these should not find fault with the climate but with *themselves*, when they fall ill. They may imagine they are very robust, "can stand anything;" but the most healthy constitution will soon succumb to imprudent exposure. "A brush of fever" often teaches a useful lesson of carefulness to the new arriver which is followed by many years of good health.

The close of the rains is said to be the most unhealthy season of the year, when the water which has spread over fields and marshes is subsiding and gives off a poisonous miasma. It is not considered safe to travel till the early part of November; from this date till March the climate is most delightful, the sky is cloudless for weeks together, the burning sun of the rainy season is now mild and quite harmless, and the nights cold enough to render a fire agreeable. The temperature throughout the year ranges from 40° to 92° in the shade, seldom in the hot season rising above the latter, or falling below the former, in the cold season, in the same locality; the lowest temperature usually occurring in January, and the highest in July; the average mean temperature is about 66°.

Europeans have lived many years in Assam without a touch of fever, others may have a fair chance of doing the same by observing a few simple precautions, *viz.*, always wear flannel next the skin, take some refreshment before going out in the morning, and never remain in wet garments except when in active exercise; when exposed to the sun, wear a large sola hat, and if necessarily long exposed, place a wet handkerchief or piece of a plantain leaf on the head; be temperate, and do not hope to ward off disease with "pegs," the slang term for a mixture of brandy or whisky and water;—it has been proved beyond question, that total abstinence is as conducive to health in India, as in any other country, and there are strong reasons for the opinion that liquors are far more injurious to the European in India than in an European climate. We, therefore, repeat the caution with emphasis: *Be temperate*, if you would keep good health.

The above remarks are applicable only to Europeans who come to the country in ordinary good health; the humid atmosphere of the rainy season and the northeasterly winds are not suited to persons of an unsound constitution. The Assamese are a weak and sickly race; fever among them is as common as are men, women and children, and as a result nearly, every one has enlarged spleen. Bowel complaints are common, dysentery carries off many, often attacking Europeans; goitre is especially prevalent about Nowgong, elephantiasis and leprosy are frequently met with; small-pox and cholera make an annual appearance, once in about five years becoming epidemic. At such times the poorer classes and opium eaters are carried off; the disease finds easy victims in those who live on the damp ground and drink water from stagnant pools and tanks, eat unripe fruit and decayed fish, and have only a thin cloth to cover them in the coldest nights.

When ill they depend on charms and incantations for recovery; to cure a sick child, a little copper tube is plugged with some root or herb, and tied around the neck or forearm by the family priest, with some "vain repetitions," or a "Bhokat" is called who fans the child with a leaf of Belongoni, a species of fern, while repeating a sloke of the shasters. The anxious mother has far more faith in these means, than she would have in the medicines of an English physician, and only when all their own methods have failed, will they resort to "belatee" or foreign medicines. They treat an ailing cow or goat much in the same manner as they do their children; a live frog is tied round its neck as a cure. It is not strange, therefore, that there is rarely a family without its buried children: the wonder is that so many survive such mismanagement.

Assistance in illness is afforded the poorer classes by the establishment, aided by Government, and by local subscription, of a Charitable Dispensary in every sudder station, where medicines are freely dispensed and patients taken in and provided for.

The native language may be embarrassing to the new-comer, especially if his first residence in India is in Assam. Government officials, transferred from other parts of India, have an advantage in having acquired to some extent Hindustanee, which is generally understood all over India. It is advisable for any one, expecting to spend some years in any part of India, to acquire Hindustanee. With some knowledge of that language no one need be speechless even in Assam; most of the Court people and the Mahomedan house servants all understand it. It is of assistance, too, in acquiring Assamese as there are many words common to both. A planter who could speak Hindustanee would be understood by most of his imported coolies.

In Lower Assam the language spoken is very much mixed up with Bengallee, but in Upper Assam it is more purely spoken, especially in the Sibsagar district, this having been the residence of the ancient native nobility.

The Assamese language has been called by some a corruption of Bengallee, but not by any one who has studied the language critically. The best scholars in the language the province has ever had, among English officials or missionaries, are of *one* opinion that it is a pure and copious language, rich in phraseology distinctively its own; like Bengallee and Hindustanee, originating in the ancient Sanskrit, there are many words common to all. Assamese is easily acquired and easily spoken; many foreigners speak it fluently who have never learned the written characters. The Alphabet does not differ from the Bengallee, except that some letters have a different sound; the most noticeable is, that the Bengallee character for *ch* is *s* in Assamese, and the Bengallee *sh* becomes a guttural *h*. The grammatical construction of the two is distinct, the syntactical similar. That the languages are quite distinct, no better

2

proof is needed than the fact, that a Bengallee does not understand an Assamese and *vice versâ.* Officers who understand Bengallee very well, are quite at a loss when they hear Assamese, pure and simple, spoken by a villager.

On this subject we need not add, but refer any one especially interested, to a pamphlet by a native, entitled "A few words on the Assamese language," &c. In it the author gives a list of ancient Assamese literature,—of sixty-two Hindoo religious works and Purans, and over forty dramatic works, having for their subject historical events found in the celebrated poems, the Mahabharat and the Ramayan. The Assamese cannot be said to be destitute of a literature.

Many useful works have been issued from the American Baptist Mission Press, since its establishment in 1837, prepared by the Missionaries. They were the first to prepare school books to aid in the promotion of education, some of which are still in use in the Government schools. Rev. N. Brown translated the New Testament into Assamese, also "Pilgrims Progress" and other useful books; he also translated and composed many sacred songs.

To aid in the study of the vernacular, a Bengallee and Assamese Dictionary was prepared by Jaduram Dekha Boruah in 1839 for Col. Jenkins, and presented by him to the Mission. "Brown's Grammatical

Notices" was issued in 1848, also a "Vocabulary and Phrase book," by Mrs. Cuttur; in 1864 a small Vocabulary in English and Assamese was compiled by Mrs. Ward, the former work being out of print. In 1867, Dr. Bronson compiled and issued an Assamese and English Dictionary.

Several useful school books have been prepared by native gentlemen. Babu Hem Chundra Boruah's "Primers" obtained a Government prize.

A monthly vernacular paper, called the "Orunodoi," or Dawn of Light, began its career of usefulness in 1846, and for many years was the only paper published in the province. For several years it was most carefully edited and profusely illustrated, treating on all subjects, both secular and religious, in a manner calculated to instruct and interest the people. This useful little sheet came to an end in December 1880.

At the present time two papers are published in Assam, the "Belashini," a monthly issue by the Aunyati Gohain, on the Majuli; and "The Assam News," recently started, is published and edited by native gentlemen in Goahati, and issued weekly, partly in English, and partly in the Vernacular.

The natives of Bengal, of whom there are a large number in all the stations, employed in the Courts and Schools, patronize Calcutta papers in Bengallee and English. The "Indian Mirror" represents the Bramo Sumaj sect, some of whom are in all the stations.

The languages spoken in adjacent tracts, and by the hill tribes, are entirely distinct and very numerous, *viz.*, the Abor, Bhutanese, Cacharee, Duffla, Garo, Hajong, Kampti, Khassee, Kuki, Lalong, Manipuri, Mech, Mikirs, Miri, Mishme, several dialects of Naga, Rabha, Singpho and Tiperah. Some of these tribes may be met with in every part of Assam, and usually the Assamese language will be found a means of communication with their chief or leader.

POPULATION AND EDUCATION.

CHAPTER III.

IT is very difficult to obtain a survey, or a correct census of Assam; the former is attended with the risk of a skirmish with border tribes, and when the necessary questions are asked to obtain a census, the people are alarmed, and suspect the Government of some secret designs.

The valley of the Brahmaputra lies between longitude 90° and 97°, and latitude 26° to 28°. To this has been added the valleys of the Barrak and Surma, comprising Sylhet and Cachar under the one term Assam, and under one Chief Commissioner. The area has been differently estimated; in 1843, Robinson's estimate of the valley of the Brahmaputra was 30,000 square miles; Dr. Hunter's estimate in 1872 was 20,683 for the great river valley, 14,447 for the hill country and 6,668 for the valley of the Barrak and Surma. The Government report for 1882 gives for Assam alone 21,414, including Sylhet and Cachar 34,941 square miles.

The population is fixed by Robinson at 800,000; by Dr. Hunter at 4,132,019 including Sylhet and Cachar, an average of 99 to the square mile. The

Government report for 1882 gives, males 2,455,852, and females 2,331,194, making a total of 4,787,046.

The population is annually increasing from the importation of laborers for the Tea Estates. From 1843 to 1883 there has been an increase of 275 per cent. in the population.

Although the country is now so sparsely populated, evidences are numerous that the province in former times supported a large population, and kings, and chiefs of great wealth. Goahati, Tezpore, and many places in Upper Assam, are strewn with the debris of former grandeur ; lofty granite pillars, stone blocks and slabs, elaborately carved with scrolls and figures in relief, are found half buried or scattered about in great numbers. King's massive brick palaces and theatres are hidden in jungle ; golden ornaments and dishes are exhumed from ancient tombs ; all these relics tell a sad story of the depletion and devastation of the past.

European enterprise is now rapidly effacing the desolation ; over vast wastes the fragrant Tea bush is spreading, and every year, around them are gathering hundreds of men, women and children from the more populous districts of India to work in the Tea gardens.

Many of the old king's highways have been reclaimed from the jungle, and are now the best roads in the country, the bridges they built over nullahs and ditches were so substantially constructed, that to the present time they are in a sound reliable condition.

The prospect for the future of the province may well inspire hopefulness, if to the enterprise of foreign settlers, is added the fostering care of a benign Christian Government, administering justice impartially to all classes, and aiding every lawful undertaking with beneficent rules; then may we expect to see a rapid advance in every thing that tends to the development of its resources, and to the improvement of a prosperous and happy people.

Great progress has been made in general education since British occupation. The present educational system was adopted when the province was separated from Bengal in 1874, and the policy is chiefly the same as that in Bengal. In each station there is an English High School, where boys are fitted for the Entrance Examination to the colleges of Calcutta; also a Vernacular and Normal School. The pupils in each of these Station-schools are numbered by hundreds; everywhere *boys* are eager to be taught, and parents as anxious to send them; on the other hand, if there is not opposition, there is decided apathy to female education; "a woman's duties are comprised in pleasing her husband and cherishing her children," this is the popular sentiment. A teacher of Arabic for Mahomedan boys is attached to the Station-schools. Why this concession to Mahomedanism in a Government that professes neutrality on religious subjects, we do not understand. The Bible is found in the school libraries, but never read in the schools; all moral and religious teaching is excluded; hence "Young Assam" is gradually becoming, like "Young Bengal," atheistic,—without any religion. Education dissipates Hinduism and offers nothing to fill the void.

Primary schools have been opened in the villages in every part of the province, the teachers receiving five Rupees a month from Government, and the boys adding something more in pice or grain. The school work is superintended by an Inspector-General, residing at Shillong; nine Deputy Inspectors, and fourteen Sub-Inspectors are located in the different districts. The Station-schools teach in the Bengallee language, but Assamese is allowed to be taught in village schools. Girls' schools have hitherto been few and small in Assam, nor have they been accorded the Government aid and encouragement necessary in the initiation of work so new and difficult; the prejudices of the people to female education can only be overcome by persevering effort, and such liberal aid as has been accorded in other parts of India.

For all India, sixty-six thousand schools for boys and girls are reported; in Assam the report for 1882 gives 1,455 for boys, and 71 for girls; most of the latter are Mission schools among the Khassias, aided by Government. There are also one or two girls' schools in Goahati, Tezpore, Nowgong and Sibsagar; at present none in the large station of Debrughur. A boarding school was started in Shillong in 1881 for European and Eurasian children, that had an average of fifteen during the year, and cost Rs. 6,954, of which amount Government paid Rs. 4,000. The average cost of each pupil was Rs. 463-9-7. The Chief Commissioner remarks, "that the school so far has been the most expensive of its class in India." It is regarded as an experiment, its continuance depending on its future success; latterly, it has been more successful, and another school has been opened for boys.

The present Chief Commissioner energetically encourages education for all classes, and doubtless will readily forward any effort to solve the most difficult problem of all, *female education*. An Industrial school for native youth is opened in Jorhat. Mr. Williamson, a wealthy Tea Planter, bequeathed two lacs of Rupees as a permanent fund for the establishment of schools for training the native young men of the province in mechanical arts, such as carpentering, smithing, shoe-making, &c. The interest of the bequest supports this school at Jorhat, also a teacher of surveying in the Sibagar Station-school. As far as we can learn, very meagre results have thus far been realized from this generous effort to raise up a class of skilled artisans to meet a crying want everywhere. There are three kinds of indigenous schools of a strictly religious character; the Hindu "tols" for teaching Sanskrit and the Vedas, the Mahomedan "maktab," teaching Arabic and the Koran, and the Kampti priests' schools teaching Budhism. The only Singpho school is about twenty miles beyond Makum.

Schools among the border tribes,—Nagas, Garos, Mikirs and Cacharees,—are encouraged by grants-in-aid from Government.

The educational report for 1882 gives an average of *one* in every one hundred and two persons attending school in the province.

Postal arrangements have greatly improved within the past few years; a daily mail arrives at the stations with great regularity from Calcutta and intervening stations. This has hitherto been performed by runners at the rate of five miles an hour, with the mail bag swung on a pole over the shoulder, with little tinkling bells attached to give notice of approach, the Queen's mail having "the right of way." In this country we fancy the *right of way* is seldom disputed except by a tiger. The runners are armed with a horn, whistle or trumpet, and as they run over a road through thick jungle, they make all the noise possible to frighten away wild animals, but in spite of this device, occasionally a poor fellow is seized and carried off by a fearless tiger. The runners go in company of two or more.

The Calcutta mail comes to Dubri by train and steamer; from there it is taken up by a squad of runners eight miles, then by another the same distance, and so on, night and day, till the last station is reached. In this way letters from Calcutta reach Debrughur in eight days. Arrangements are now complete that will further expedite the mail. A small steamer starts *daily* from Dubri and Debrughur, dropping the mail as she passes the landing points on the river, occupying four days in the upward and three days in the downward trip. She can accommodate a few cabin and deck passengers. This is a great boon to the province; besides the advantage to the mail, there is an opportunity to visit Calcutta and return in one-fourth the time of the regular steamers.

The foreign mail service has equally improved: formerly we had only a monthly mail, and considered ourselves highly favored over former times; now a mail from England and America arrives *weekly* with great regularity. The English mail steamers drop the Indian mail at Bombay, whence it is taken by train across the country to Calcutta. The mail for Assam leaves the Calcutta train at Sahibgunge, whence it is taken to Caragola, thence to Jalpaiguri, and on by train and steamer to Dubri. An Inspecter-General of Post Offices visits each district annually; there are also subordinate officers located in each district. Orders from the Head Department in Shillong are lithographed for circulation.

The head offices of the Assam circle are Dubri, Goahati, Shillong, Tezpore, Nowgong, Golaghat, Jorhat, Sibsagar and Debrughur.

Branch post offices have multiplied for the accommodation of Tea Planters. Many employ a private postman to go between the gardens and the nearest post office.

We must not omit to mention the great convenience conferred by the postal department in the introduction of the money-order system and the recent improvement in returning a receipt; also the opening in 1882 of the post office savings bank, a measure tending to the well-being and thrift of the people. Hitherto, the only way they could dispose of their savings was to spend it on heathen rites, or on jewellery likely to be stolen, or resort to a common practice of burying it in the ground, often so secretly, that in case of death it is lost altogether. Since the bank was opened, depositors have become numerous, indicating that the plan has the confidence of the people.

In the march of improvement in this out-of-the-world country, the establishment of telegraphic communication must be noted. The speaking wires were first stretched from Calcutta to Goahati in 1869, but did not reach Upper Assam till about seven years after. From the main offices, branches connect Goahati with Shillong, Golaghat with Kohima, Sibsagar with Nazerah, Debrughur with Makum. Neat brick houses are erected at each station for office work and for the accommodation of the operatives. Their pay ranges from Rs. 20 to 200 a month. A message can be sent to England in four hours from any point. Telephones are becoming quite common in the province.

CHARACTERISTICS.

CHAPTER IV.

WITH regard to the character of the people not much can be said in praise; among the high caste there is considerable intelligence and outward morality, but generally the people are ignorant, indolent, and wanting in moral principle or conduct.

Their peaceableness and timidity make them a comfortable people to live among; in Burmah, to be safe from robbers, every door and window must be secured with double bars and bolts; in Assam the European may sleep in perfect security with doors and windows wide open, a privilege not to be despised in a hot country.

Another trait certainly commendable, is the kindness shown to indigent relatives. We never find an aged person, a widow or an orphan, having relatives, who are unprovided for, and in nearly every large household there are some such dependants. However poor these relatives may be, they seem willingly to share their living with the unfortunate. Native gentlemen, with only a small salary from Government, generously provide for a large number of dependants. It would surprise their English neighbours if they knew what a large portion of the man's income was consumed, not on his own wife and children but on a host of relatives. Those who have means spend lavishly on heathen festivals, and make a display of generosity in feeding the poor or in an expensive show of devotion to one of their numerous deities. An educated native gentleman has no faith in the gods he sets up for the worship of an ignorant crowd. The light imparted by even secular education dissipates the idolatrous superstitions imbibed in his childhood, but he has a host of heathen friends who are pleased with a manifestation of devotion to the gods of his fathers, and for this reason alone many strictly observe, *outwardly*, caste rules and continue the *forms* of Hinduism before their friends.

The people are generally polite and respectful to their superiors: a native passing a European on the road closes his umbrella, or if riding, dismounts. Respect for superiors is carefully maintained among themselves; a low caste man may be seen bowing to the ground before a Brahmin.

The respect natives pay to English officials often amounts to cringing obsequiousness, especially if any favor is desired, their devotion and humility is expressed in terms of oriental extravagance. To the ordinary inquiry, "Are you well." They reply, "*Hozuror onugrohor duarai bhale asun.*"—By your honor's favor I am well—they often say. "You are a god and what cannot you do?" "*Hozure mur ai bupai,*"—You are my mother and father—are common expressions of confidence from a native to a European. There is no idea of sincerity, of course, in such language. Sincerity is foreign to native character; self-interest is the ruling principle under a show of humility and regard. Falsehood is universal from the oldest to the youngest, in fact, they are so much in the habit of lying, that they sometimes neglect to tell the truth when it would be for their interest to do so. The Courts of Justice are hot beds of lying, bribery, and perjury among the natives. How it is possible for the English officials to decide what is true and what is false, and be sure of administering justice among such a people, is a problem difficult to solve. The people are very litigious and "mokodama kori,"—prosecute—for trifling causes. The cases with which the Courts are always full, are largely about land boundary and debts, but the most numerous are about *girls.* Troubles arise from the pernicious habit of parents betrothing their children in infancy, and binding the agreement with presents of value; years pass over the heads of all parties, circumstances change, and the parties change their minds; the girl is perhaps refused, or given to another man, or she may be enticed away: in any event there is a case in Court.

The dishonest character of the people is a fruitful source of litigation. It is not natural, scarcely *possible*, for them to do a straight-forward transaction; there must be deceit somewhere, some device for taking an unfair advantage, some knavery to keep back part of what is due, and any number of lies to get the best of the bargain. Too timid to be house-breakers or highway robbers, they are adepts at petty pilfering; servants ostensibly provide for themselves, but they lose no opportunity to do this at their masters' expense. They purchase supplies, but not without a share for themselves; their "memsahib" (lady) may daily deal out from the store-room the needed supply, but no fear that the wily servant will not somehow circumvent her carefulness. Servants are necessarily Mahomedans, as caste prevents a Hindu from serving Europeans. They always prefer serving bachelors, where they generally escape careful supervision, and their opportunity is better for feathering their own nests.

The minds of European children left to the care of servants become fearfully contaminated with the native deceitfulness of character. Sometimes they are taught worse things, and only after the mischief is done, some day the fond mother is shocked to hear the sweet lips of her darling utter a *lie* or foul words that cannot be repeated. The pollution may be deeper than she suspects, though her fears may suggest to her the divine truth that "out of the abundance of the heart the mouth speaketh.' 'The reason is obvious why watchful parents hasten their little ones out of the country, fearing far more the baneful influence on their minds than the physical effects of the climate, and thus subject themselves to many long years of painful separation.

That native character is much improved by the influence of European residents, would not be admitted by the Europeans themselves. The means of exerting a good influence is wanting; the natives are very conservative, and they are held aloof at such a distance from all English society, that they never know each other except as Englishman and native,—the ruling and subject races; of course, the ruling race is treated with great respect, but there is no venture on social grounds. The higher classes, and especially those who have had an English education, would be greatly benefited by some social intercourse with English-speaking people; as it is, they have no opportunity to air their knowledge of the language in conversation, consequently they are embarrassed in the use of it, make many absurd mistakes, and use highflown words that subject them to ridicule. We have rarely seen a brief note from a native gentleman in correct English.

"PANI KOLO." A WATER JAR OF
COARSE EARTHEN-WARE IN COMMON USE.

Hindus are *religiously neat;* the daily bath before eating must be observed by every caste from the highest to the lowest, and their garments washed. Religiously compelled to take their food on mother earth, the ground where they eat must undergo a purifying process, in their estimation, which is performed by some female member of the family or servant. This consists in washing the ground over with cow-dung and water, giving it a smooth clean appearance; to them the odour never seems offensive, as the cow is held sacred by the people. This process of "lipping" is the daily routine in a Hindu family, and as necessary a preparation for the family meal, as laying the table among Europeans.

Strict Hindus of the higher caste never eat in the same garments they wear at other times. The male members of the family eat first, the women and children afterwards; they eat with the right hand and only from brass dishes which are kept carefully scoured. Their meal is a large platter of rice, a small bowl of vegetable or fish curry, and a cup of water for each person.

The cooking must be done by one of their own caste; poor people cook for themselves, but the high caste employ a 'Takur,'--a Brahmin servant, and if for any cause he is absent, the Babu's wife or some member of the family must do the cooking, for on no account would the Babu taste food prepared by any one below his own caste.

It is in vain to attempt any detail in this brief glimpse, of the rules and restrictions caste imposes on the people ; it is an element that enters into everything they do, subjecting them to much suffering, and depriving them of much enjoyment. It is difficult for a European to understand the tenacity with which the poorest man will cling to his caste ; it appears to be dearer to him than life ; he is as unmoved by money as intimidated by threats : to be an outcaste from his home and friends, cannot be endured. This feature of Hinduism is the greatest obstacle to improvement of any kind. Christianity is loosening its fetters all over India, and by a power more than human these chains will fall.

Mahomedans are not restricted in their diet by caste, but eat anything they choose, except pork. The most commendable feature of Mahomedanis mand Hinduism, too, is the prohibition of the use of all spirituous liquors ; no strict Hindu or follower of the Prophet will taste liquor ; many of the former do so however secretly, and among the latter many servants are drunkards. Nearly all Europeans in India drink liquor in moderation, having been accustomed to it in the " old country" ; but natives have not the strength of character to keep within the bounds of moderation the limitation: broken and the taste acquired, they are ruined. Many call themselves Christians, simply on the ground that they have lost caste, and can eat beef and drink brandy; these bring disgrace on the entire Christian community, being taken as specimens of the class. We know of no missionary who receives a person into the church merely because he has thrown off the restraints of caste. That feature of heathenism which forbids the use of liquor, it would be well to engraft on the Christian church, and not liquor *ad libitum* as natives now seem to suppose, bringing disaster on the native Christian church.

The veryprevalent habit of eatingor smoking opium in Assam is not less to be deplored. In 1860, at the suggestion of General Jenkins, native cultivation of opium was prohibited, that Goverment might have entire control of the trade, and possibly lessen the consumption. Prior to British occupation, it is said it was largely consumed. At the present time just outside the boundary, at tho base of the hills, acres of opium are seen in cultivation. It cannot be said to have been *forced* upon the people as a source of revenue, though in 1864 fifty-three per cent. of the revenue was realized from opium. A rise of price has not materially affected the consumption; the people have more money than formerly, and the miserable victim of opium eating will go without food willingly, but he must have his "Kani." He will not work for food and clothes for his wife and children—*they* may starve—but for the poisonous drug that puts all his faculties in a state of stupor and makes a half dead animal of him. Knowing its demoralizing effect on the people, ought not some measures to be taken to arrest the growing evil? Government might lessen the temptation to its use by gradually reducing the quantity imported year by year till brought to a minimum. At present a drawback of one-half to two-thirds of the wages received by the people from Tea Planters is received by Government for opium.

MANNERS AND CUSTOMS.

CHAPTER V.

ASSAMESE are so extremely indolent, we never find among them the nice handicraft that abounds in other parts of India. They cultivate just sufficient to meet present necessities, leaving the future to be cared for when it comes. Hinduism makes them stolid fatalists : if disease carries off their cattle, floods drown their crops or draught withers them, an afflicted man with surprising coolness, points to his forehead and remarks, "mur konpal beya,"—my fate is bad—whatever fate has written on his forehead must come to pass. If he is sent to jail for crime, there is no consciousness of personal guilt and ill desert; he is simply the victim of fate in his own estimation. Any one will readily acknowledge the binding obligations of the Ten Commandments, but if he breaks any of them, it was his *fate*, he cannot help himself, he thinks it will be atoned for by suffering in this, or some future state ; his religion gives him no real sense of moral obligation, no idea of individual responsibility, no sense of sin and its deserved punishment, opens no way of salvation except by personal suffering, and offers no hope of future happiness except it is wrought out by his own meritorious deeds. Dark and hopeless as such a religion is, they cling to it with a tenacity, similar to that with which they cling to their primitive ploughshares, wooden pestle and mortar and *grindstones*,—the heirlooms of generations,—thoroughly satisfied to live and die as their ancestors have done.

Here and there a few have caught a glimmer of a purer faith and brighter hopes, through the preaching of the gospel of our Lord Jesus Christ and the free circulation of portions of the New Testament, besides tracts full of gospel truth distributed among the people; and, evidences are not wanting of an awakened interest in the truths therein contained, although any innovation upon ancient customs must be a slow and gradual work, while any hope that the abundant resources of this beautiful valley will ever be developed, except by foreigners, is utterly futile.

The people are primitive in their habits and costumes; the introduction of English society affects but slightly the costume of the men. Those who hold Government appointments generally wear shoes and stockings, some wear trousers, with the native style of jacket, and some young men wear the entire English costume. Women keep strictly to the style of past centuries, which is simple, economical, and well adapted to their mode of life and the climate. The native costume of men is a strip of white cloth or

WOMAN CARRYING A JAR OF WATER IN ASSAM.

silk so arranged around the waist, that the folds flow to the knees; a long sleeved tight fitting jacket and about five yards of thin white muslin around the head completes the costume.

Mahomedans usually wear a cap. Coolies while at work wear only a small waist cloth.

The women's costume is a skirt cut like a pillow-case, about the same width, open at each end; sometimes they are made of cotton cloth, but usually all classes wear the native silk. The top is drawn tightly around the waist, and a twist of the fold tucked in, keeps it on, without other fastening; a a short sleeved jacket is worn, just meeting the skirt at the waist; a silk scarf is passed over the left shoulder, then around the waist, the ends of which have a gay border hanging in front. When going out, a white sheet of cloth or muslin three yards long and one and a half wide, called a "Chudda," is placed simply over the head, one end flowing, the other tossed over the left shoulder. This garment is never worn by children. Nearly every family has its hand loom placed under the eaves of the house, where the women busy themselves between the morning and evening meals, weaving silk and cotton cloth garments for the family, and often some pieces in addition to sell to pay their taxes. "Markin" cloth, as American sheeting is called, is in very general use for common wear by men and women. The "Gamosa," or handkerchief (though it does not correspond in use with the English article), men usually carry with their money and "Tamul Pân,"—betel-leaf and its adjuncts, tied in the corners, in a coarse home spun cloth, with a border and fringe at the ends.

The women also weave heavy warm sheets from the floss of Moga silk, or from the "Eri" silk in which they wrap themselves in cold weather.

The native substitute for an umbrella is a broad rimmed hat, called a "Japi," made of bamboo finely woven over palm leaves, which is serviceable in sun or rain; of late years the English umbrella has come into general use.

In the management of the expenses of a family, the wife enjoys a large share of woman's rights; her husband puts his income into her hands, and she uses it very much as she pleases, often buries a portion in the ground as a reserve for future use. A favourite way of spending surplus funds, is in buying jewellery of which they are very fond; often the entire wealth of a family consists in a horde of jewellery, which is brought out only at a marriage. An apparently poor man, at such times, often makes a surprising display of wealth. Native jewellery is very unlike the ornaments worn by English ladies;

the ear ornaments are gold or amber plugs, to be inserted in a hole in the lobe of the ear about an inch in circumference and two inches long; the forward end is set with rubies and emeralds. The necklace is a string of glass beads of gold, and coral alternately, and pendant from the middle, is a barrel shaped gold ornament set with precious stones. The ornaments for the hair are various devices of flowers and pendant ornaments in silver and pearls. Bracelets and armlets are of silver or gold in successive rings, or made three or four inches broad, set with precious stones, and fastening with a clasp. Diamonds are not seen, except among the wealthy.

Natives report that there is a mountain in Assam where diamonds are found. Assamese never wear anklets, nose rings, or toe rings, as is common in Bengal. Tea garden coolie women are often seen with neck, arms, and ankles loaded with brass ornaments.

Family attachment among the people is very strong; sons are the idols of their mothers, they lavish their affection upon them, every wish is gratified and faults seldom corrected. If sickness, accident, or death befall them, they are plunged into the deepest grief, and indulge in oriental extravagance in their expressions of affection. In a loud agonizing cry, that can be heard by all her neighbours, the mother mourns, "O my moon of gold, my star of silver, my necklace of pearls; jewel of my existence," with accompanying gestures of deep emotion, beating the breast and tearing the hair. The great respect paid to the aged in native society and in the family, is a most commendable feature of domestic life among the people. A grandfather or grandmother is the acknowledged head of the household; though there may be others in it advanced in years, his or her authority is supreme with every member of the family. Filial reverence is expected from grown up sons and daughters, and any conduct to the contrary would be considered brutal.

Among the praises awarded to a deceased native gentlemen was his exemplary filial love; it was said of him "he obeyed his mother like a docile child, even *adored* her; for twelve years before his death he was in the habit of drinking the water *sanctified* by the *foot-dust* of his mother." This is not an unusual way of showing adoration; Hindu worshippers drink the water in which a Brahmin has washed his feet. In the Puran it is enjoined upon a wife "to wash the feet of her lord and drink the water." We cannot say how often this is obeyed, but we know that the respect a wife pays her husband often amounts to abject fear. When he makes his appearance she draws her "chuddah" over her face, or runs away; she cannot meet him in the presence of any visitor; she never utters his name, only speaks *of* him as the father of her eldest son or daughter, if there is no son, she never sits when he stands; she is in no sense the companion of her husband. Among the high caste their apartments are quite distinct; he has his verandah or parlour where he receives his friends, his spacious bedroom where he lounges, reads and smokes; but quite shut off from glimpse of all this by high walls, are rooms where his wife and children and maidservants draw along a monotonous existence.

Children are the delight of a woman's existence; a childless woman feels herself under the curse of some evil demon, and many are her penances and prayers to avert the calamity.

Mothers usually suckle their infants till two or three, and sometimes till five years of age. *Boys* are sent to school when six or seven years old, but the projudice against female education is so strong, that it is with difficulty they can be gathered into schools. Among the high caste, objection is raised to sending them through the public streets; among working people the mother asks, "Ki labh"? "What is the profit? If my daughter reads and writes, she can never get Government employment." Another objection we often meet is this, "If they learn to write, they will be writing on the sly to the boys and go to the bad." We are silent when this comes up, feeling the force of the argument among such a corrupt people.

Much has been accomplished in overcoming these prejudices in other parts of India, and the fact that there is at present a girls' school in Sibsagar of over fifty pupils, is a fair indication that Assam is falling into line.

Among the high caste we often find a woman who has learnt to read by a little teaching from her husband or son, but among the low class we very seldom find a woman who can read. They are mostly in a low state of ignorance and depravity; no better evidence of this is needed than to hear a woman in temper abuse her antagonist. Such scenes usually occur outside the house, often in the road, in the hearing of a score of men, women and children. The two women stand at a distance from each other, and at the top of their voices, with various violent and disgusting gestures, they both together pour forth a volley of the vilest "galli," abuse, a foul-mouthed woman could be capable of uttering, quite shameless in regard to the number or sex of the listeners.

Children, never slow at learning what is evil, soon become adepts in the use of "gali" when in temper with their playmates. They are never taught to control their tempers, much less their tongues; the only hope of an improvement in the race is the diffusion of *Christianized* education.

DOMESTIC EVENTS.

CHAPTER VI.

EUROPEANS, though they may have been many years resident in India, have a very limited opportunity to know much about the private habits and domestic ceremonies of the people. When a wedding occurs, they hear the din of tom-toms, the clanging of cymbals, the gunfire of bursting bamboos, and the general hullabulu of a crowd of men and boys who always disgrace such an occasion. The only part of the affair the public witness, is a procession on the road of men, women, and children, dressed in their gayest, following the bridegroom, who is seated on an elephant, distinguished by a peculiar gay turban, and a little in the rear, a "Dhoolie" in which the bride is hidden. A "Dhoolie" is canoe shaped, in fact a short dugout, gaily painted, suspended by the ends on a pole, by which it is borne on the shoulders of two men. Over the pole a gay cloth is spread which conceals the occupant. The procession is accompanied by a band of musicians, who make anything but music, by fingering a dozen drumheads and beating as many cymbals, the chief aim seeming to be to make all the noise possible.

We will now take a glimpse of the less demonstrative part of the affair. "Kama" the Hindu Cupid, is represented as a handsome boy, sitting astride a parrot, surrounded by maidens who bear aloft a banner on which is pictured the "mahara" fish ; in his hands he holds a bow, made of flowers, the string is a row of bees ; in one hand he holds five arrows, typifying the five senses. What his particular duties are in pairing the sexes we are not informed, as *love* has no place in the preliminaries of a Hindu marriage, though we believe it as often succeeds the event as in other communities where the reverse is true.

Among the lower classes there is no zenana seclusion, and the young people can see each other, but the choice is arranged by the parents. Among the high caste, the young girl is kept in seclusion and a love story is an impossibility. Usually, while the children are in their infancy, a contract of marriage is made between the parents, ratified by valuable presents, and often by a sum of money to the girl's parents. This is attended by some ceremonies by the family priest, and a feast for their friends ; this is called the *sota beya*, or little wedding. A "Gutuku," or go-between, is usually employed to obtain the consent of the parties, and he cunningly represents to each that the alliance is everything that can be desired, and after a deal of talk, he arranges what presents and what amount of money must be given for the girl. This man also pretends to be an astrologer, and divines under what star the event will be auspicious. In the Sheva Purana the following description is given of a *perfect* Indian beauty. "The girl was of a yellow color, had a nose like the flower of a sesamuna, her legs were taper like the plantain-tree, her eyes large like the leaf of the lotus, her eyebrows extended to her ears, her lips were red like the young leaves of the mangoe tree, her face was like the full-moon, her voice like the sound of the cuckoo, her arms reached to her knees, her throat was like that of a pigeon, her loins narrow like that of a lion, her hair hung in curls down to her feet, her teeth were like the seeds of a pomegranate, and her gait like that of a drunken elephant." Ugliness is never an obstacle to the marriage of an Indian maiden; handsome or ugly, every one must be married; a *spinster* is an unheard-of person in native society, and would be considered a disgrace to a family. An instance is related of several girls being married to an aged Brahmin as he was being taken to the river to die, to remove the disgrace of being unmarried! A Kulin Brahmin may have several wives, but polygamy is not common. The girls married to a dying man would be subjected to the cruel laws of widowhood, forbidding them to wear ornaments, or fine garments and making them the slaves of the household, having to perform the most menial service.

There are three marriage cremonies, the first when the contract is made between the parents ; the second is the great wedding, when the boy and girl meet for the first time and look each other in the face.

Among Brahmins, a boy may be married after he has been invested with the *poitre*, or sacred thread worn over the shoulder ; this is performed at ten years of age, the girl is married at from seven to ten years of age. Preparatory to the event, the astrologer consults the marriage horoscope, and decides on the auspicious day for the ceremony. For several days previous, the bride and groom elect are subjected to various purifying rites, such as bathing and anointing with turmeric. The boy must hold in his hand for four days and nights the betel-nut scissors, the girl the box of paint for her eyelids. At the house of each party, relatives gather and are feasted. The night preceding the wedding, musicians with drums and cymbals fill the air with a horrible din ; the noise is not confined within a house, but is in the *sontal*, the yard, which is kept clean for various purposes. Here the family sit at evening and receive friends ; for this occasion, it is temporarily roofed over with plantain-leaves, and often tastefully decorated with cut paper hangings.

On the morning of the wedding-day, prepared cuds of betel-nut are sent to their friends; this is the *invitation card* to the wedding. For a further insight into the proceedings we will quote the description given by a native girl * of the bride's dress and the ceremony on the marriage of her cousin :—

" Towards the evening of her wedding-day Mohimi was bathed in rosewater, her feet and hands dyed red and she was dressed in a red silk 'saree' (the saree six yards long forms both skirt and chuddah), embroidered with gold with a golden border; on her head was an elegant ornament of gold, richly wrought and set with jewels, a fringe of gold and pearls hanging over her forehead; from the forehead another similar band passes across the parting and joins the back hair. The ears pierced in six places, were loaded down with earrings of the most exquisite workmanship, some so long that they touched her neck, while the loops of others were three inches in diameter. A necklace of pearls clasped her throat, and besides this, a dozen chains were around her neck, each longer than the one above and of different patterns. Both arms were covered with armlets and bracelets above and below the elbow. Passing four times around the loins, was a very heavy gold chain, fastened by a massive gold buckle set with

* Kardu.

precious stones. She had as many as a dozen silver bangles on each ankle, some falling over the foot as far as the toes; these were edged with a fringe of small silver bells that made a soft tinkling noise as she moved. If Mohimi had been obliged to walk, the weight of her jewellery would have been burdensome. All this jewellery was given to her by her father as a dowry. While the priests are giving a set form of instructions to the father-in-law, the gentlemen of the house sprinkle the guests with rose-water, a little silver box is passed among the higher class of guests containing an exquisite perfume into which each one dips his finger—Brahmins being always *first* served.

"About midnight the cry is heard 'The bridegroom comes!' several little girls under six years of age, go out with lighted torches to meet him. On arrival he is seated on a handsome mat in the middle of the court. He is dressed in a waist cloth of dark purple silk, and on his head is a high cap of silk and gold tinsel; soon he is called into the house, and the relatives are also admitted to the ceremony, and the *door is shut.* He stands like a statue in the middle of the room; a man blows a trumpet and five women appear, all closely veiled, each having a tray on her head; the first is the bride's mother, who carries red hot coals in her tray and a pot of water in her hand, the other women have various kinds of fruit in their trays. They pass round the bridegroom seven times, the mother spilling the water in a circle around him; at the seventh time, when behind the groom, she suddenly throws the tray of burning coals on his head: they fall at his feet. She then turns the tray wrong side up and stands upon it, and with her hands closed together, she touches his forehead, lips and chin, with oil, plaintain and salt, then moves away. Now the bride appears, closely veiled, seated on a board on which a variety of figures are chalked. She is carried seven times around the groom, then placed at his feet. She is then raised to a level with his face, a sheet is thrown over their heads, and they are permitted to look at each other for about five minutes. The sheet being removed, they are seated opposite each other in the idol worship room, on a circle elaborately chalked on the floor, and between them a case filled with flowers on which the back of the groom's hand is placed, and the back of the bride's hand is placed in his; wreaths of flowers are now bound around their hands, and ten rupees placed on the top for the priests. Mohimi's father and one of the priests seat themselves in front, the father holding a silver dish of Ganges water in which is a beautiful ruby ring, and a thin iron bracelet; the ring is given to the groom, the bracelet to the bride, then the water is sprinkled on them and the flowers thrown at them. Mohimi is lifted up and carried first to his right side, then to his left, then a corner of the garment of each is tied together, and they are pronounced *man and wife.*

The ceremony ended, the groom goes among the men, and the bride among the women.

Wedding festivities are usually continued through the night; professional dancing girls amuse the people, sometimes native dramas are played, drums are kept beating, sweetmeats and "Tamul Pân" are passed around; the men are never weary of the "Hookah," or "hubble-bubble" pipe.

After the wedding, the bride goes to her mother-in-law's for a visit of a few weeks, but she rarely sees her husband during the time; she is but a child now, and must return to her father's house and remain till the age of maturity, which in this country is at twelve or fourteen years of age. At this time the final marriage takes place, which is a quiet ceremony, after which she goes to her husband's home to remain permanently. Her future happiness depends far more on her mother-in-law than on her husband; she sees little of him, but is entirely under the control of her mother-in-law. She takes away all her jewellery, and she can have it to wear only when it is *her* pleasure. She is obliged to remain in the women's apartments, and is never the companion of her husband. This description of a wedding cannot be folo wed out in all its details by the poorer classes, but as far as means will allow, the main features are the same with all classes of Hindus. The heavy expenses of the marriage ceremony is the chief reason why daughters are not welcome in a family. The sin of infanticide is rarely visited on a boy. The expensiveness of weddings is one of the evils of native society; many involve themselves in debt at such times, that hangs like a millstone round their necks for the rest of life. The cruel laws to which widows are subjected is another evil that calls loudly for a change in public sentiment, sustained by the strong arm of the law, to overcome. The widow must never marry; she may be a mere child, bereaved of one called her husband whom she may never have seen, and for whom she can feel no sorrow, but she must wear for *life* the coarse garments of widowhood; she must eat but one meal a day, she must fast two days in each week; not even a drop of water must pass her lips, however thirsty; she must perform the most menial services of the house, and in every way her life is made so miserable, no one can wonder that the "suttee" (widow immolation) found many votaries: death was preferred to such a life. Suttee has disappeared in the light of Christianity, and its attendant evils must have a like fate. Any one observant of the progress of events, must note the gradual change which the influence of a Christian Government, combined with the earnest labors of those Christian men and women who live in India only for the present and eternal welfare of the people, has already wrought in sweeping away the darkness of heathen superstition, in loosening the fetters of caste, and in lifting the ignorant and degraded into the knowledge and liberty wherewith Christ makes free.

At the present time there is a growing public sentiment in favor of reform of some of the ancient customs in Hindu society—a sentiment against zenana seclusion, against child-marriage, against expensive weddings, in favor of widow marriage, —and these sentiments are being boldly acted out.

We must now turn our attention from the merriest occasion in life to notice the customs of the saddest; marriage and death are the most important events in every family the world over, the two are connected in every Government report and in every newspaper. Every nation has its own customs in regard to the dead. The funeral customs of a hot country must necessarily be briefer than in a cold; here, burial, or cremation, takes place within a few hours of dissolution. Mahomedans always bury but cremation is the orthodox method among Hindus except in the case of very young children. The Ahoms always bury their dead. If death takes place where fuel is high-priced, and the friends are too poor to provide a funeral pile, the face of the deceased is blackened with a wisp of straw, the body weighted with a stone, and thrown into the nearest river, soon to be devoured by sharks or alligators. Poor coolies at the gardens without relatives, are simply wrapped in a mat and borne off to the jungles, and if buried, it is done so slightly, that they soon become food for jackals. It is not strange therefore, that such a mystery as death should be enveloped in superstitious fear in the minds of an ignorant people ; the house in which a person dies no one will occupy, it must be dismantled or burned. To prevent this, if possible, the dying person is taken out into the open air to die. To touch the dead is pollution, and only men of the same caste as the deceased, can be prevailed on to bear the remains to burial or cremation. No change of dress is ever made to indicate mourning.

The "Shradho"—mourning ceremonies—must be performed by the eldest son ; if there is no son, then by the nearest male relative. It is considered a great misfortune to have no *son* to pray the souls of their parents out of the Hindu purgatory. Near relatives perform the *Shradho* at every annual return of the day of decease.

The rich spend large sums on funeral ceremonies, in making offerings, and feasting and feeding the Brahmins. Sandal wood, and other costly perfumes, are burned on the funeral pile; clarified butter and pitch are added to increase the flame, while the priests are repeating their *Muntras*. If the person is a man, his face is placed downwards; if a woman, upwards, the head towards the north. The burning takes place on a river bank, and after the pile is consumed, the remainder is thrown into the river.

One often hears the loud lamentations of the women on the death of a relative; their distressing cries can be heard all over the neighbourhood; not simply crying, but loudly expressing their grief in the most pitiful and extravagant terms, at the same time tearing their hair, striking their forehead, beating their breasts, and flinging themselves about, expressive of the greatest agony. The death of a child, the mother thinks the work of some fiend whose only object is to distress her; she knows nothing of a Father's hand that only chastens for her good; in her religion, there is no ray of hope, all is dark despair. At one time she is breathing out curses on the imaginary being she thinks the cause of her trouble, at another her mouth is full of praises of the lost one : she mourns that her lap is empty, it is her *fate*, written on her forehead, and her heart sinks into leaden hopelessness. With what joy would her face light up, if told of the beautiful home above for all Christ's little ones, and of the bright hope that it is possible to meet her loved one again.

LOWER ASSAM.

CHAPTER VII.

DUBRI, the first station on entering the province of Assam, has been built up and become a civil station only since the Northern Bengal State Railway from Calcutta reached Kaunia, on the opposite side of the Brahmaputra. It has drawn off from Goalpara, the next station above, the Government officers, and reduced that to a sub-divisional station with only one officer. A small steamer plies between Dubri and the Railway terminus, for the conveyance of passengers and luggage. This route considerably shortens the time between Assam and Calcutta. Passengers can go from Calcutta to Dubri, or *vice versâ*, in twenty-five hours, while by river steamer, *viâ* Goalundo, requires four or five days. It is *this* that has given importance to a very small place; from the steamer, judging from the number of nice bungalows in sight, one would think it a large place, but a short walk will reveal the fact than you have seen it *all;* the station is only a narrow strip of land, almost an island, and the space so limited, that the buildings are quite near each other. A resident, describing the proximity of his neighbours, remarked that "he could stand in his own door and shoot peas into the door of any of his neighbours"; we do not suppose he ever so far compromised his dignity as to try it.

The native town of Goalpara clusters around the base of a high rocky hill; the bungalows on the hill are now mostly deserted, the officers having removed to Dubri, and the American Baptist missionaries having removed to Tura on the Garro hills. It is a place of considerable trade with the lower proinces. Less tea is grown here than in any other district; but there is a large amount of other cargo taken by boats and steamers, which is brought from the interior, principally, mustard seed, dry chillies, and lac. The lac is exported in its natural state, encrusted on twigs of trees by an insect, "Coccus Ficus."

A larger number of native boats are seen here than at any station, employed in running up small streams and bringing down produce in bulk, which is here bagged and shipped in large boats running to Calcutta, or on steamers.

A traveller starting from Goalpara on the Trunk Road, passing tea gardens and Cacharee villages, travelling a distance of ninety miles, would arrive at the sudder station Goahati. (*goa* is the Assamese for betel-nut, and *hati* is a mart) Betel-nut trees are numerous in the district, and the large trade formerly carried on in these nuts gave the name to the place.

It is distinguished, however, for other things; it was the seat of royalty during the splendour of the Assam dynasty, and a strongly fortified town, with many costly buildings, the debris of which can now be seen, are scattered about the station.

After British occupation, it was the residence of the chief officers of Government till 1873, when this honor was transferred to a more healthy location on the Khassia hills.

Goahati lies, a crescent formed by rocky spurs of the Khassia hills, jutting out into the Brahmaputra at each end, about two miles long on the river side. The station has a pleasing appearance; near the bank are seen the chapel and bungalows of the American Baptist Mission, and further up, the Government buildings, church and officers' bungalows on the river side, then undulations of hill and valley, dotted with Tea bushes, give variety to the pleasing scene. We would suppose the station one of the most healthy, on account of its location on the river, but the contrary is the general opinion. Epidemics have raged here fearfully; in 1852 cholera carried off one-third of the population. Undrained swamps at the back of the town are supposed to be the chief cause of the insalubrity of the place.

This district is noted for its numerous temples, and sacred resorts for pilgrims. A temple on the opposite bank called Kamrup, gives the name to the district. The hill forming the north-western boundary called "*Nila Chul*," or blue mountain, has several noted temples built to "*Kamaikya*," the goddess of love or lust. These temples are visited by pilgrims from all parts of India, and in former times the monasteries were filled with priests and nuns; no less than five hundred women, it is said, "were consecrated to the temple service, whose filthy songs and more obscene dances attracted crowds of people to the midnight orgies; a song was not tolerated which did not contain the most marked allusions to unchastity, while those that were so abominable, that no person could repeat them, received the loudest applause. All this was done in the very face of the idol, nor does the thought, "Thou God seest me," ever produce the slightest pause in these obscene revels. Though, doubtless, this description was quite true under Hindu native administration, we think it cannot be applicable to any scenes now enacted; such demoralizing revels surely would not be tolerated by a Christian Government any more than infanticide or suttee. It is very little, however, that Europeans ever know of the unutterable abominations of heathenism, or the polluting idol festival that attracts crowds of natives which usually fills the midnight hours. A short time since we visited the temples of Kamaikya, but we saw no nuns, and though a festival day, there were few visitors; it has certainly lost its former prestige, everything indicating decay, except the small temple that crowns the summit. Here we found a devotee from Upper India, a tall thin man with a fierce expression of countenance, his forehead marked with red and white spots and crescent stripes, the Brahminical thread over his shoulder, and the Fakeer string of beads in his hands. Here he lived alone, attending upon the few worshippers who brought their gifts, or a goat for sacrifice. He came here about two years ago on a religious pilgrimage, and finding the place neglected and the temple going to ruin, he set about begging money to repair it, and succeeded in obtaining a sufficient sum; now the white sugar loaf shaped temple, with its golden pinnacle, glistens in the sun-light and attracts attention from a long distance.

Before British occupation, human sacrifices were not uncommon at these shrines. Several large temples on the western side are said to be built on the site of a former Budhist temple of great grandeur and gigantic proportions. There are evidences of the truth of this in the quantities of granite blocks scattered over the hill, cut into pillars, plinths, and cornices, of great size, which are beautifully carved in relief, with figures, flowers, and scrolls. The paths leading to the summit on the eastern and western side, are paved with these stones ; an idea may be formed of their number from the fact that this stone stairway is from twelve to fifteen feet wide on the eastern side and it takes an hour to ascend the hill, which is eight hundred feet high.

Another temple of equal note is situated at Haju, about six miles from the northern bank of the river, on a hill 300 feet high. The idol, "*Mohamuni*" is highly venerated, strange to say, both by Brahmins and Budhists ; the latter believe their great prophet's presence has conferred a sacred efficacy to the spot; hence Budhists, from their distant homes in Thibet and China, travel for weary days and weeks the pathless Himalayas, to lay their burdens of sin at the feet of this idol shrine, firmly believing in its efficacy. While passing Goahati a small rocky island in the middle of the river attracts attention, a temple is seen among the trees and a lighthouse on a projecting rock erected by the late General Jenkins. Formerly peacocks were very numerous on the island, hence it was called Peacock island, but since a sand bank has connected it with the station, the birds have left. It is considered a sacred spot by Hindus, who believe it was formed by the god "Sib" from the dust which had marked his forehead. The temple shrine of "***Hanuman***" the monkey-god, is a favorite resort of the Kaiyahs, emigrants from Marwar, who are worshippers of *Hanuman.* The population of Goahati is about 11,500, a large proportion of whom are Mahomedans. The boys' schools are noted for their excellence. English service is regularly held in the church by the chaplain, or in his absence by one of the Government officials, and Assamese service is held in the Mission Chapel, at present conducted by an ordained native preacher.

Shillong, the residence of the Chief Commissioner and other head officers of Government, is situated on one of the Khassia hills about 5,000 feet high with a climate so salubrious, and scenery so grand and beautiful, that it has been termed "the paradise of Assam." The carpets of violets, buttercups and daisies, the birds, fruits and flowers, are cheering reminders to those who are strangers in a strange land of a dear far-away home.

The tedious journey to this delightful spot is a serious obstacle to an invalid enjoying its advantages; a distance of sixty-seven miles must be made from Goahati by riding, or by "Tonga," a two-seated cart drawn by ponies, or by bullock train: the latter occupying two days; by Tonga ten or twelve hours. The road is said to be a model of engineering skill. There are also eight other roads connecting Shillong with hill towns. The location cannot be considered a favourable one for Government officers to become acquainted with the Assamese race, or their language, the Khassia language being quite distinct, and allied to the Indo-Chinese. Tezpore, the sudder station of the Durrung district, on the north bank of the river, presents an appearance of three hills on the river side, each topped with a bungalow: by a short walk around the hills, the scene opens upon lakes and tanks, and a clean green lawn on which are situated the church and the Government buildings, the bazar and native houses occupying the roads running north-east and west. Carved granite blocks, remains of former grandeur, are piled up on the lawn.

On the north boundary of the district stretch the mountain ranges of the Bhutias, Akas and Duphlas. The latter tribe formerly caused disturbances that led to a petty war with Government, but of late years they are peaceable. The Akas are at the present time giving the Government occasion to send an expedition against them.

At Mungledye, a town south-west of Tezpore, an annual fair is held, at which large quantities of hill produce and manufacture are brought for sale or barter; also numbers of the sturdy ponies for which Bhutan is noted.

In this district, a tract of country called the Chalguri division, is inhabited chiefly by Cacharees, a hardy, industrious race, physically superior to the Assamese consequent on more active habits and liberal diet. We must not leave Tezpore without special mention that this place has been the home of the *discoverer of Assam Tea,* Mr. Charles Bruce and family, for the past thirty-five years. His name deserves to be held in honor in the province, as the originator of an extensive industry that has already enriched thousands, and worked wonders in the development of the resources of the country. Government very tardily rewarded him with a free grant of 3,000 acres of waste land. The old gentleman reached the *Better* land about ten years ago, but his widow survives with heart and hope, ripe for a heavenly inheritance. Four sons and a son-in-law are Tea Planters in the district.

Nowgong lies directly opposite Tezpore, thirty-two miles inland from the river steamer landing place, Koliabar. It can also be reached by boat on the river Kullung, which traverses through the north side of the district, and empties into the Brahmaputra above Goahati. At Koliabar there is a Telegraph office, the only one near the river between Goahati and Debrughur.

Nowgong is a clean kept level plain with Government buildings, offices and mission bungalows scattered over it; the native population skirting the plain.

The country lying low and level, the climate in the hot season is extremely stuffy. The rural population is numerous; villages lie thickly on both sides of the Kullung. Large quantities of betelnut, pân-leaf, sugarcane and silk are produced; the rice crop exceeds that of any other district. Tea gardens are numerous.

The Mikeer hills skirt the division on the south, and the Raha division, inhabited by Lalongs, on the west. These two hill tribes far outnumber the Assamese. The next landing places of the steamers above Koliabar are Negriting, and Dhunsiri-mukh, each of which connect with Kohima, the Government station recently formed on the Angami Naga hills. The former is the nearest direct road for travel, the latter for the conveyance of luggage and commissariat stores on account of the convenience of river communication up the Dhunsiri to Golaghat, a subdivisional station of the Sibsagar district. Both these places have been made lively by the recent Naga campaign, having been the landing places of officers, regiments of soldiers, scores of bullocks, ponies, mules, and elephants, and all the various appurtenances of war.

The Government station is on the spur of a hill, 300 feet below the Naga village of Kohima; a Deputy Commissioner, a Surgeon, and half a regiment are stationed there; since the close of the campaign peace has been maintained. The height of the hill is nearly equal to that of Shillong, and the climate and scenery comparable.

Golaghat derives its importance chiefly on account of its connection by road with Kohima.

Jorhat, thirty-five miles southwest from Sibsagar, connects with the steamers at Kukula-mukh, ten miles distant. At the time of British occupation it was the seat of native royalty, and has since been the place of residence of the deposed royal family. During the Mutiny of 1857, the son of the late king and a few adherents, had plotted the murder of all the English and the resumption of authority, but fortunately a friend to the English Government divulged the plan just in time to prevent Cawnpore horrors from being enacted in Assam. The secret was made known to Colonel Holroyd, then Deputy Commissioner of Sibsagar, who with surprising skill and alacrity nipped the whole scheme in the bud; while feigning to his servants to be very ill in the house, he was pushing rapidly for Jorhat with a few armed men during the night, and on arrival surrounded the house where the would-be king was, demanded admittance, and without parley made him a prisoner, had sent him off to Calcutta, thus bravely saving Assam from being a sharer in the horrible scenes of the mutiny, at the same time indicating how wide spread was the spirit that instigated them.

UPPER ASSAM.

CHAPTER VIII.

SIBSAGAR, the sudder station of the district by the same name, is connected by road with the Brahmaputra at Dikho and Desang-mukh ; the former distant seventeen miles in the rainy season, and twenty-two in the dry season, from the steamer landing when the river is low. The latter is only eight miles from the station, but the road hitherto has been only a path through the jungle in the dry season and impassable in the rains ; now, however, Government have made a liberal appropriation to render it passable all the year round.

Sibsagar has an urban population of about 5,000 in an area of seven square miles ; the station is by many considered the prettiest, and one of the healthiest in Assam ; the chief feature of beauty and interest is Sib's ocean, as the name of the station implies, —Sib, a Hindu deity, and Sagar, meaning ocean. This is a beautiful artificial pond, two miles square, excavated in terraces, quite shallow near the bank, and a square in the centre very deep ; the rainfall and evaporation keeps the tank full, and the water fresh. It was excavated with forced labor during the Assamese dynasty.

At about the same time three temples dedicated to Sib were built on one side the tank, with the exception of a dark arch in the centre for the idol shrine; these are solid brick structures, the centre and largest one is surmounted by a large acorn shaped tip, thickly plated with gold, that can be seen from a long distance, the height being about 200 feet; the bullet holes in it indicate that numerous attempts have been made to *loot* the gold. Near the base is a facing of carved stone slabs, representing different Hindu deities. These massive structures are probably more than a century old, and the only injury that threatens them is the growth of trees from seeds dropped in the interstices of the solid masonry. To preserve them, Government have these annually cut away. Before the hideous stone image of Sib, in the dark arch, you can always see a small light glimmering like a distant star, but Christian feet must never approach nearer than the doorway.

The people hold many superstitious notions about the tank; they believe there are golden turtles in it; *ordinary* turtles are often caught in it, and fine large fish with hook and line, or spears.

No bathing or washing is allowed in it, that the water may be kept pure for drinking purposes.

In the cold season large flocks of wild geese settle on the tank in the morning, and about four o'clock, with a loud rush of their wings, they all swoop off to the Brahmaputra.

The bund of this lovely pond furnishes a high airy situation for the Government buildings, and for the bungalows of the European residents; the situation is quite distinct from the native part of the town. The bazaar lies along the bank of the Dikho, half a mile from the tank. Some of the residents have boats and enjoy a row or sail on Sib's ocean at evening, and the unoccupied temple-land is the lawn tennis game ground.

On the opposite bank of the Dikho are the ruins of the ancient capital, Rungpore. The Ronghor, or theatre of the Assam king, is a two-storied massive brick building that may defy the decaying hand of time for centuries; not far from it are the ruins of a palace with lofty gateways, and huge stone blocks, with representations of the feats of the gods cut in relief on them, scattered about; numerous dungeon-like underground rooms suggest the idea that they may have been intended for political prisoners. Near by is "Joysagor" tank about the size of the one in Sibsagar; also two smaller tanks surrounded with jungle.

About nine miles southerly another royal palace lies in ruin, surrounded by a brick wall, two miles in circumference, with lofty gateways. The district is especially rich in such relics of the past, having been the residence of the Ahoms of rank, some of whose descendants are now living near Jorhat.

Nazerah, the packing and forwarding station of the Assam Tea Company, is situated on the bank of the Dikho, about ten miles south of Sibsagar, and communicates with the river steamers at the mouth of the river.

The Lukhimpore district compiises the whole of the north-eastern extremity of the province on both banks of the Brahmaputra ; it is separated from the Sibsagar district by the river Lohit, and extends to the confines of the hill tribes, that separate it from Burmah and China, the boundary not being well defined. It is the most sparsely populated part of Assam.

The British assumed control of this part of Assam in 1839. The district is rich in coal, petroleum and limestone. Gold washing was farmed out by the Assam kings, but of late years the people are content with the *silver* they get at the Tea gardens, which are numerous in this district. There are two famous places of pilgrimage in this region ; the "Brahmacund," a circular basin in a narrow gorge of the Himalayas, near where the Brahmaputra turns from its southerly course to a south-westerly; the other is the "Deo Dubi," a dark pool of great depth through which the Desang river leaves the Naga hills. Although the journey to these places is both difficult and dangerous, they are supposed to have an odour of sanctity that, if breathed, will confer a blessing on this life, and that to come; annually hundreds of poor sin-sick souls endure the hardship and fatigue of a visit to these sacred places.

Debrughur, the civil station of the Lukhimpore district, and the terminal point of the river steamers, through the impetus given by the recent railway enterprise, has become the largest station in Assam. This enterprise was started in 1881 by a few Tea Estate proprietors, and anticipates completion in 1884. The road runs from the steamer landing north easterly to Doomdooma, then southerly to Makum, a distance of sixty miles from Debrughur; especially to reach extensive coal fields on the Naga hills, which are expected to be immensely profitable. The road is ultimately to extend north from Doomdooma to Sadiya for the convenience of the Tea estates.

Government for a score of years have had similar work under consideration, and now give substantial aid to the enterprise; it is hoped, they will be aroused to complete a long contemplated plan of extending the railway from Dubri northward through the province.

The projectors of the railway propose to extend it on from Makum over the hills to Burmah, to facilitate re-opening the old trade route between Assam, Burmah and China.

The subject of reopening the route has been discussed by the British Association, the Chamber of Commerce, and by Government for some years without practical result. Several gentlemen have explored the route enduring great hardships and danger; Messrs. Cooper, Sladen, and more recently Colquhon have made extensive explorations, and one of Assam's most scientific Tea planters, S. E. Peal, has also contributed valuable information about these unknown regions from personal research. Government are reluctant to take any measures likely to disturb the peace with the border tribes.

Recently a new plan has been presented for opening the route by C. H. Lepper, F. R. G. S. and M. R. A. S., which proposes to avoid collision with the neighbouring tribes by using the Singphos as go-betweens from Assam to China. The Mishmees are uncompromising, the Khamptees are hostile, while the Singphos are peaceably disposed and occupy a neutral territory. The route, *viâ* Makum to the Irrawaddy, is said to be quite feasible, none of the passes exceeding 2,500 feet above sea level. The plan meets with the approval of many interested in the object; at present it is under consideration by the Governor-General and Home authorities, and it is hoped they will so far sanction the scheme, as to make an appropriation for the expense of an expedition to prove its practicability.

The Singpho country was the probable route of the Ahom invaders in the thirteenth century, and also more recently of the Burmese.

It will be readily admitted that it will be of incalculable advantage to all the interests of the province, both private and public, if the route was made safe for traders and emigrants, the sparseness of the population, which is the greatest obstacle to the prosperity of Assam would thus be overcome. If the way was fairly open to the swarming villages of industrious and ingenious Chinamen, vast tracts now covered with dense jungle would soon wave with grain, or be enlivened with flocks and herds, and Tea estates would be supplied with labor and saved the heavy expense now incurred in bringing it from distant parts of India. It is impossible to estimate the value and importance of the articles of export that might be available; enough, however, is known to interest every good friend of the country in an effort to open out communication with our eastern neighbours.

Mr. Bryers, Engineer-in-Chief of the Cachar and Assam Railway Survey, has succeeded in finding an excellent route through the hills from Katigora to Pemding, practicable with fair gradients, at a reasonable cost, that will enable a railway line to be carried up the Dhunsiri valley to Golaghat, with a branch northward to Nowgong, thus giving Assam direct railway communication with both Chittagong and Calcutta.

Coal is found in several places in Assam, but the fields at Makum yield a superior quality, equal to the best British coal. It comes to the surface in seams varying from five to forty feet in thickness ; the deposits have been traced for thirteen miles, and the yield is inexhaustible. The mines are now being worked under superior overseers from Italy and North Wales, and immense quantities are now being stacked ready for transportation. The coal fields are but three miles from the Dehing river, and besides the train, boats are available to convey the coal to the steamers.

Great difficulty has been experienced in obtaining labor to work the mine. An effort was made to induce the Nagas to work ; they came ; one looked into the black hole and drew back ; he would not go in there, "*Bhoi lage*,"—afraid ; another stooped down, and peering in, shook his head, and others with the same result ; no money would tempt them to enter the "Devil's hole." Labor not being available in the country, six hundred coolies were brought from Raniganj, men accustomed to mining in their own country. Also sixty English navvies were brought from Birmingham with a superintendent, and were located at Makum

Petroleum springs, and forests of excellent timber, are within the concessions made by Government to the "Assam Railway and Trading Company."

An attempt was made to work these petroleum springs by Mr. Goodenough in 1866; a free grant was made of some hundreds of square miles, a large amount of plant and apparatus was brought to a site near Makum, but difficulties of transit, and Mr. Goodenough's death, closed operations. Now, that railway transit has been provided, doubtless the effort will be renewed.

There are iron mines in the Naga hills, and silver mines in the Kamptee country, but little is known of them except the bare fact. Members of the border tribes in this district, Mishmis, Singphos, Kamptees and Nagas, are often seen in Debrughur in the cold season, with burdens on their backs, brought for trade. Various efforts have been made to open friendly relations with them by the Government.

Dibrughur can boast of having the prettiest church in Assam; a church of England chaplain is stationed there, and a regiment of soldiers with its officers.

Sadiya, sixty-two miles north-easterly, and Jaipur thirty-five miles south-easterly, are sub-divisional stations of the district.

Tea planting is a growing industry in this district, converting a vast extent of waste and desolation, into fragrant gardens. Planters have done much in opening out roads, and in improving the means of travel, aided by Government appropriations, but that there is still great need of improvement to make travelling comfortable, is evident from the forcible illustration given in the following description of a journey in the district. "Most people are aware that it *rains* in Assam, and that when it rains, it is *wet.* But it is impossible to understand how very wet it is, how utterly waterlogged the country becomes without personal experience of travel during the rains. My attention was first attracted to the real state of affairs riding along the high road from Sibsagar to Debrughur, when sundry long poles erected here and there by the road side elicited a query as to what they were for? "To enable mahouts to keep their elephants on the road during the rains," was the reply. As at the time of the query, I was riding on a "grand trunk road" raised in some places as much as ten feet above the surrounding country, I may be forgiven for having rejoined in the pet Debrughur phrase, "Bar sells, you can't pull my leg with that yarn." But my friend was not chaffing me, it was a solemn fact; during the rains, that "grand trunk road" is, or was, often submerged under *x* feet of water, and but for the poles, the elephants might get off the embankment and have to swim for it. I will not assert that many of the main roads are thus amphibious in their habits, but a good deal has yet to be done before communication can be said to be on a firm footing in many parts of the country.

When main roads in comparatively civilized districts are so unreliable, what can be expected in that benighted place North Lukhimpore? A short sketch of a two day's journey, performed, I am delighted to say, by deputy, may give a faint idea of the fun of travelling after heavy rain in the out of the way corners of Assam. During the height of the rains such a journey as is here described would be impossible; all the troubles here met with, were merely the result of the "*chota barsat.*" (little rains). Ben, my deputy, on this occasion, with his invariable knack of getting into difficulties and out of them, again started with a companion in June, to travel from Joyhing to Pithalipam; leaving the former place after breakfast, they were boated across what had a few days before been an ordinary stream, but which was now a sheet of water extending from the Joyhing stables to the lines of the nearest garden, at least half a mile: indeed, the said lines were gradually being submerged and their removal to a higher site was in hand. The road from here to Sinatolia was above water, so the two adventurers mounted their ponies and travelled on gaily till their first difficulty was encountered in the shape of a curious bridge; this had

STRIKING ILLUSTRATION OF A D. P. W. BRIDGE.

formerly been a bridge of regular habits, not given to eccentric conduct, but the rain had demoralized it completely, and it was now a floating bridge, an island in the middle of the stream it was supposed to span, anchored by a few canes and bamboos to the posts whereon it formerly peacefully reposed. Caution and perseverance enabled the travellers to wade out to this island, and from it again to the land beyond without any serious accident, though J's pony put his foot in it, and nearly broke his leg.

A ride of a couple of miles up to the girths in water, another bridge successfully negociated,—a rotten one which gave under the ponies at every step, this time for a change, and some three or four miles of decent road beyond the station of Lukhimpore, brought them to Pitikagan and to a full stop *pro tem.* Before them stretched a great sheet of water, while the syces (grooms) who had been sent on before on the other side, said it was impassable for horse flesh. But there was a gleam of comfort in the intelligence, (only it turned out to be false) that one of the elephants was on the other side waiting to convey them on to Koddom. Hailing a rickety apology for a dugout, they spent half an hour in agony with the fear of a watery grave before their eyes, and finally reached the high land again on the further side in safety ; but never the ghost of an elephant, of course, was there. They wanted badly to go back and kill those mendacious syces, but were afraid of tempting providence any more by recrossing in that second-hand coffin, so they postponed the funerals, and trudged on manfully with hearts full of hope and boots full of water.

The prospect was not exhilarating ; four miles to go, no end of ditches to cross, and a suspicion rapidly deepening to a certainty that all the bridges were gone.

It was even worse than they imagined. A few hundred yards, and they found themselves wading up to the waist *on the road*, and they only found out, where the ditches came in, by the sudden deepening of the water, so sudden as to take them by surprise, developing a swift current, and the necessity of swimming vigorously till they could feel bottom again. Swimming fifty yards in clothes and boots every quarter of a mile, as a change from wading the intermediate distances, is not half such good fun in reality as it looks on paper, at least, so Ben says, and I am willing to take his word for it without personal experience.

In one place J. was submerged so suddenly, that he lost his head for a moment and was nearly swept away down the stream. Naturally they found this excitement a trifle monotonous and tried cautious

circuits when they came to deep places, thereby avoiding swmming, but entailing extra wading till at last they were completely done up and could hardly move.

Fortunately at the last stream, a very deep and rapid one, the elephant hove in sight, and at last they reached Koddom where they remained for the night.

There was anxious discussion that night whether the journey should be continued; they had come over the *best* half of the road, and the shortest; before them lay any number of miles of a fair representation of the Kosmic chaos before the land was separated from the water. Sleep, after the fatigues of the day, overtook them before a decision had been reached, and morning and rest brought renewed courage, and a fresh start was determined on. Although there had been heavy rain during the night, the waters appeared to be subsiding off the face of the earth, so taking all that was left in the way of provisions,—some cold potatoes and three eggs, they packed their bedding and portmanteau on one elephant, mounted another, and started.

The Koddam river is a broad and rapid stream, but Ben says he had no idea how deep it was till he saw the luggage elephant, wading on ahead of them, suddenly disappear: the tip of his trunk coming up for breath, and the head of the mahout bobbing round, being the only signs on the surface of the water of where a moment before was a big elephant and all their luggage. The ship had gone down with all its cargo, but it sailed along in its peculiar fashion under the water and climbed up the opposite bank all right again, though the freight was rather *moist ;* the bedding was all pulp, the portmanteaux were visibly swelling with the moisture they had imbibed, like the Tea drinking ladies at the Brick Lane Branch Association, and water was pouring out of Ben's despatch box, speaking eloquently of the state of the papers and records within. But while noting these things more in sorrow than in anger, their attention was suddenly attracted to themselves; J. was submerged up to the neck, and Ben intently gazing on the ruinous state of his property and forgetting to hold on, found himself off on a separate voyage independent of the elephant on which he had taken his passage. A grasp at a friendly loose rope brought him up in time, and he floated on board again minus his umbrella which he had up at the time he was washed overboard, for, of course, it was raining. They got across to "soundings" eventually, having swallowed a good deal of water from the lurching of the elephant as he swam across, and though no water poured out of them, as it did out of the boxes, they were very wet. For the rest of the journey they perferred taking boats across unencumbered, but boats were few and streams numerous, so even if the sun had come out, which it didn't, there was no danger of their getting dry. At the next stream they found a boat, or they would probably had to wait till the dry season set in. Before venturing on this inland sea they had breakfast; one of the eggs proved—well, if they could not count that chicken before it was hatched, they could before they ate it, so one egg, and a few cold potatoes each was the cheerful meal with which they regaled themselves; a cheeroot made life worth living a little longer, and then away they walked about a mile through shallow water to where the boat was; transshipped their impedimenta from the elephant to the ark, and set off on a three mile's voyage. They landed at length on the high bank of the Subasiri river and resumed their quadrupedal progress; still they had a long way to go, plodding on now through long heavy grass which switched pleasantly in their faces, and then wading through deep water, till as the shades of night were falling fast, they found themselves nearing their destination, but with still one deep stream to cross. Here a new difficulty awaited them; the elephants worn out and disgusted with swimming refused to face the deep water, tumbling, rolling, backing, and shaking their heads at it, despite the efforts of the mahouts to force them on. The passengers had to jump over board to avoid being shaken off, and standing in water over their waists, waited till the the mahouts had licked the nonsense out of their heads. They were then ferried across, one at a time, in fear and trembling. Ben went first, and there being no dry ground to stand on, landed on the fork of a tree while the elephant went back for J; but when he arrived, the elephant thought one passenger was enough for him for the rest of the journey, and obstinately refused to come under the tree to take Ben on board again. He managed to make a jump for it at last, but he says he never before fully realized what being "up a tree" meant, till he was shivering in the fork watching the elephant slashing round and insisting that he had not got a ticket beyond that station. This was fortunately the last of it. A little more wading brought them to the end of their journey, at eight P. M., after thirteen hours of it in the rain, into the water, and *vice versâ.* They had to borrow clothes and wrap themselves in blankets, and a good dinner made them oblivious of their troubles, and, strange to say, neither of them got fever which is the most marvellous part of the story. Ben says if he were married to a mermaid at the bottom of the deep blue sea, he couldn't be any wetter than he was the second day: in short, that he will never be a "wetter un."

INDUSTRIES.

CHAPTER IX.

We will glance only at what natives busy themselves about, leaving the *great* industry of the province, Tea planting, for separate consideration.

If we consider the sparseness of the population, and the consequent limited area under cultivation, we will find the industries of the Assamese not to be despised. In this jungly country, a farmer or ryot, as such are termed in India, cannot settle in an isolated situation, with a wide stretch of fields around him, as in more civilized lands: the people must huddle together in a village for mutual protection from wild beasts that abound in the country. Every man must have his cow-house, granary, and garden, *close* to his dwelling, the rice fields are a stretch of several acres of low swampy land, not far from the village, which they all share in cultivating; they often share each others' possessions in cattle for ploughing: a man ploughs his neighbour's field, for the use of the animals on his own.

Rice cultivation is the farmers chief industry but not many are sufficiently industrious to do much more than suffice to supply his own family, and pay his taxes. His implements of husbandry are of the rudest and most primitive kind, his ploughshare is a bit of iron about four inches long, and one and a half wide, fastened to the end of a tree branch with a bend or knee in the middle. The ploughman lays hold of the upper end to guide the plough, and in the other hand holds a stick with which he constantly goads the oxen with a cry of "He, he," "He, he;" now and then giving the animal's tail a cruel twist to urge him on. A bamboo pole is attached to an equally rude yoke that draws the plough along; with this little blade he scratches the ground over three or four times; if heavy rain falls, he is better pleased, and continues to follow the plough, knee-deep in mud and water.

In June and July the seed grain is thickly sown in a small patch near his house, and when a foot high, it is pulled up, tied in bundles, the top ends cut off, and carried to the field by the men of the family for planting out.

The rice field is divided into square blocks by a "dhap,"—mud thrown up a few inches high, to keep the water standing around the plants.

The planting, which occurs in August is done by the women with an alacrity we never see them display in anything else, holding a bunch of plants in one hand, with the other they take a tuft of several plants and stick it in the mud, then very rapidly another and another, placing them about a foot apart, in rows, while walking through the slush.

In fields near the jungle, a small staging is erected, roofed with thatch, where a watchman remains during the night to keep away wild animals ; when he hears any approach, he shouts and yells to frighten them away, and if this is not successful, he lights a wisp of straw and flourishes it towards them. Wild boars, buffaloes, deer and elephants often come to the fields, and sometimes the watchman is shaken from his high perch and killed. Rice fields require no weeding or irrigating in this well-watered country.

" Are there not four months and then cometh the harvest ? " The latter half of December, and the first half of January are the golden days, when there is not a cloud in the sky, and the air cool and refreshing, then the reapers go forth with sickle in hand ; these are the women again, usually going in company, taking their little ones with them.

The sickle is the same as was used in ancient times, a small hooked knife about nine inches long ; with this they clip off a tuft of grain stalks (leaving most of the stalk) dropping it on the ground as they pass along ; men are usually in the fields sharing the work, they bind the sheaves and bear the grain home, tied to the ends of a pole which is swung across their shoulders. Harvest is followed by " Behu, " a harvest home festival, when there is general feasting and visiting among friends.

As in Bible times, "the ox treadeth out the corn," so here, in primitive Assam, this is the custom, but contrary to command, the ox is usually muzzled, the grain is spread on the threshing floor, and the patient ox walks round and round over it, till his hoofs have separated the grain from the stalks; then it must be winnowed, which the women do, dexterously tossing it on a bamboo pan; "the chaff the wind driveth away." The grain is stored in a "Bohral,"—a bin the size of a small house with a raised floor, built of bamboo and plastered with mud to make it tight; frequently grain is stored on the stalk, and threshed as required.

After threshing follows the slow tedious process which the women go through to separate the rice from the husk, and clean it for cooking. In an outer shed a mortar is set in the ground, and a pestle fixed in the heavy end of a long lever, which is balanced on a bamboo rest placed about two-thirds of the length from the pestle. A woman treads the lighter end of the beam, while holding in her hand a long stick with a cloth swab on the end, with which she pushes back into the mortar the grain that flies out when the pestle strikes; most likely there is a baby swung in a cloth on her back while at work. The pounding is followed by sifting and fanning, and picking, till finally the rice is ready for washing and cooking. Considering the amount of labor required in preparing rice, we may be surprised that it can be sold at *one* anna a seer, or one cent and a half per pound.

Rice is the chief food of the people ; the ordinary amount for a full grown person is one pound at a meal, eaten with a little fish or vegetable curry. A Hindu is a thorough vegetarian, never eating meat, unless a duck or goat that has been offered in sacrifice. The women are more industrious than the men, the poor especially, have very little spare time, their rice cleaning, cooking, weaving and care of children, keep them busy ; they often complain "*boohoot kam,*" plenty of work, "*ahori nai,*" no leisure : this is their excuse for not learning to read and for not reading when they know how to ; little girls taught to read at school and early removed to do home-work, or to be married, often forget all they have learned from having no home encouragement to look at a book.

The luxuries the Assam ryot cultivates is a patch of sugarcane, another of mustard seed, for the oil with which they cook their food, another of *dhol*, a species of small pea of different kinds ; also a few tobacco plants, and the different kinds of spices used in making a curry. Every garden has some betel-nut, palm trees, and *Pan*—a spicy leafed vine that they eat with it, and invariably, plantain trees.

The juice of the sugar cane is pressed in a rude machine; a huge mortar is hewn on the top of the trunk of a tree, with a hole at the base to let the juice out; a small tree trunk is the pestle, to which is attached a long lever; at the end of this the patient ox is yoked and walked round and round the mortar. The juice is boiled down to treacle or dark brown sugar, put into coarse earthen pots holding about a pound, and sold in the bazar from two to four annas each.

One of the chief industries of the people is silk culture and manufacture, in which the women are the principal workers.

There are three varieties of silk-worm, the Eri, Muga and Pat. The Eri worm, Phalœda Cynthia is reared within doors, and fed on the castor oil plant; in some places, where this is not abundant, on some jungle plants; they require constant feeding and attention, as they must be kept from rats and insects, with which every house is pestered.

This silk is spun into a coarse thread which is woven into large sheets, worn over the head and shoulders in the cold season, or for a night blanket; common garments are also made of it as it, is very strong and durable.

Muga silk is a speciality of Assam, the cloth is woven of the thread in its natural color, and is much thicker and stronger than the tussar silk of Northern India. The silk is in common wear by both sexes and all classes. The raw silk in skeins forms quite an important article of export.

The Muga Moths, " Antherœa Assama " are reared in a " Sum " tree forest, the ground underneath the trees is kept clean, the more readily to find any worms that drop off ; this species give five breeds in a year, from the first and the last, the best silk is produced ; 50,000 cocoons is a good return from an acre of forest, yielding twelve seers (25 lbs.) of silk, worth, at present prices, from sixteen to eighteen rupees a seer.

The labor and expense of keeping a forest is trifling, but great care is necessary in the breeding season ; the forest must be watched by day, to keep away crows, and other birds that devour them, and by night, to keep off owls, bats, and rats. To keep ants away, before placing the worms on the trees, the trunk is daubed with treacle to attract them, and when collected in great numbers, they are burnt.

The process of rearing is thus described. After the cocoons have begun to form, they are put into a closed basket, and suspended from the roof of a hut ; the day after they are hatched, the female moths are taken out, and tied to small wisps of thatch, taken from over the fire place, its darkened color being thought more acceptable to the moths; these wisps are then hung on a string suspended across the house, to protect them from rats and lizards. Morning and evening they are taken out and exposed to the sun. The eggs laid the first three days are the only ones considered worth keeping; ten days after the eggs are laid,.when a few are hatched, the wisps of straw, to which they had been fastened, are hung on the trees on which the caterpillars are to feed. To prevent them coming to the ground, fresh plantain leaves are fastened around the trunk, over the slippery surface of which they cannot crawl. When about beginning to spin, they come down the trunks where they are collected in baskets and put under branches of dry leaves; into these they crawl and form the cocoon. The total duration of a breed is from sixty to seventy days. The cocoons are not easily killed; they are put over a slow fire and boiled for an hour in a solution of potash. The instrument for winding off the silk is the rudest imaginable; a thick piece of bamboo is split in halves, and the pieces driven into the ground two feet apart; on a projection of the joints a stick is laid, to which is fixed a round piece of board a foot in diameter; a rotatory motion is given by jerking this axle on which the thread winds; in front is the vessel holding the cocoons, from this a stick is placed horizontally for the thread to travel upon. Two women are employed, one attends to the cocoons, the other jerks the axle with the right hand and directs the thread up the left forearm, so that it is twisted in coming down towards the hand; the left hand directs the thread over the axle. Twenty cocoons are usually wound off in one thread. The thread is made into skeins of one or two rupees weight. A woman's skirt, two and a quarter yards long and one yard wide (in the piece) is worth from four to six rupees; a man's suria,—waist cloth, six to eight yards long and one yard wide, is worth from twelve to eighteen rupees. The silk of the natural color is a dark straw color; the bright colors forming the borders of their scarfs are cotton. The silk of Lower Assam is of coarser and stronger kind, from the worm being fed on the "Hualoo" tree; the Sum is only found in Upper Assam. The cocoons are brought to Upper Assam to improve the breed, but they only last one year. The worms when fed on the "Chapa" tree, produce a beautiful silk called Chapa putea. The "Pat," or mulberry worms, Bombyx Mori," indigenous to China are raised only to a limited extent in Assam; they require constant attention within doors, but the silk produced is very beautiful, white, fine, and soft. The cloth woven is expensive and worn only on special occasions. The skein silk is sold at twelve rupees a pound, and the cloth by weight, with the added expense of weaving. Another kind of beautiful silk is made by the Muga moth fed on the Mezenkuri or Addakuri tree, the woven silk is called ***Mezenkure*** silk, and demands a price quite equal to the mulberry worm variety. The silk is very white and soft, and sometimes embroidered with gold or silver, and especially chosen for a bride's dress.

The "Deo Moth" "Atticus Atlas" is grandly large and beautiful, the breadth from tip to tip of the wings measuring from ten to twelve inches. No use is made of the cocoons.

The mechanics of Assam are very unskilful; goldsmiths are numerous, but their work will not compare with that of other parts of India.

Carpenters, blacksmiths, and shoemakers are equally unskilful; most of the good work of this kind in Assam is done by Bengallees. There are a few who do fair work as carvers of ivory.

The makers and vendors of sweetmeats, and the washermen, are all from other parts of India.

In Lower Assam there are braziers, who pound out the coarse brass plates and cups used by the people.

Potters mould with their hands earthen water jars, small pots for the native made sugar, little saucers used for lamps, pipes, bowls, &c., but all the work is of the coarsest kind.

The stills and grogshops are run by Bengallees, and they are the chief customers; a cheap liquor is made from rice, and from treacle; these sinks of ruin, licensed by Government, are found in every station, and near the Tea gardens, robbing the coolies of their wages, and tempting them on the way to misery. Planters have often protested against these places being planted at their doors, as dangerous to the peace and comfort of their people, but in vain. Assamese *women* do most of the petty trading; the regular evening bazar, held in every station, is entirely in the hands of Mahomedan women, except the fish vendors, who are dooms. The men do the fishing, but only the women *sell* the fish. The little shops that lie all along the bazar roads, are tended only by women, the men are off on other work.

In every station there are a few "Beparis," emigrants from Dacca, who deal in dry goods, tinned provisions, &c. The Kyahs, who are found in numbers in every station, are emigrants from Marwar; they are the money-lenders, and bankers, and the most enterprising traders in the country.

TEA CULTIVATION.

CHAPTER X.

TEA cultivation in this province has rapidly become the chief industry of the country; through European enterprise it has spread over more than four score thousand acres within a few years, and at the present time gives employment to more than six hundred European managers and assistants, and two or three hundred thousands of laborers, and is the main support of two lines of steamers running weekly to and from Calcutta.

The beginning, however, was small, slow and doubtful, like the "cloud as big as a man's hand," the most sanguine never imagined to what it would grow, and neither the Central nor Local Government were prepared for the rapidity with which the news, that there were vast tracts of Tea land available for cultivation on easy terms, fired the ambition of fortune seekers; "gold diggings" were never invested with a greater charm, or more golden dreams of "castles in the air" than these wild jungles of Assam to the rush of Tea planters. It cannot be denied that a few realized *all*, and some, even *more* than all their brightest dreams, at a time when speculation ran highest ; but these cases are exceptional, far the greatest number have been forced to see their air castles vanish, and many are still struggling with the difficulties of the work, with the hoped-for fortune still in the misty distance.

A glance over the two score years of the history of the rise and progress of the Tea industry may be of interest to our readers.

No fanciful legend gives romance to its origin in Assam like the following, told of Tea cultivation in China :—

"Confucius, the Great Chinese reformer, having registered a vow to the gods that he would keep awake seven days at a stretch, found its execution more difficult than he expected ; all possible means were employed to keep his eyes open, but on the seventh day he fell asleep, when he awoke and found he had broken his vow, he exclaimed " Vile traitors !" I shall prevent you from ever closing again ! Cutting off his eyelids, he threw them away. The pitying gods made the Tea bush grow where the eyelids fell, in order to assist future devotees in their exercises." The keep-awake property of Tea is too well known to make it doubtful as to the success of future devotees, and we will turn our attention to the matter of fact way Tea planting began in Assam.

Of old, the tribes on the northern border made

use of the indigenous Tea plant themselves, also for purposes of trade with the Bhuteas. They manufactured it in a rough way, simply drying and packing it in large bamboos, a seer of Tea (2lbs.) bringing from ten to twelve rupees at Lassa.

When the news was first promulgated that indigenous Tea was found in Assam, the idea of cultivating it for trade with the people in the north was urged as an important incentive; this plan of the projectors has not yet been realized, but the prospect was never so bright as at present, that the trade route will soon be opened to the tribes north and east of Assam.

In 1823 Mr. Robert Bruce, a merchant, learned from a Singpho Chief that Tea was growing wild in the northern part of the province, and he exacted from him a promise to send him some plants and seed, which was not fulfilled. The following year when his brother Mr. C. A. Bruce, who was in charge of a division of gun-boats at Sadiya, the Sinpho Chief again appeared, and this time fulfilled his former agreement and sent Tea plants and seed.

Mr. Bruce sent a portion of these to Mr. David Scott, the Governor-General's Agent, and the remainder he planted in his own garden. Mr. Scott sent some to the Botanical gardens, which were favourably reported on. The importance of the subject does not seem to have awakened an interest in Lord Amherst, then Governor-General, and not till 1834 when Lord William Bentinck became Govenor-General was the subject taken up with earnestness by the Central Government. His Lordship brought the subject of the cultivation of Tea in various parts of India before the Council, and a Committee was appointed to devise a plan for its accomplishment.

Mr. Gordon was sent to China to procure plants, seed, and Chinamen, to commence Tea operations.

During his absence the Tea Committee received communications from Col. Jenkins, the Commissioner of Assam, also from Lieut. Charlton and Mr. Bruce, placing the report beyond a doubt that the Tea plant was indigenous in Assam. This was followed by the appointment of a deputation of three scientific gentlemen, Dr. Wallich and Asst. Surgeons McLelland and Griffith, to proceed to Sadiya, in November 1835, for scientific research.

Dr. Griffith, whose reputation ranked high as a Botanist, reported his conviction that success was certain to Tea cultivation, on the ground that the Tea plant was indigeneous ; also that there was great similarity in the configuration of the valley and in the climate to those parts of China, the best known as Tea producing.

At the suggestion of Col. Jenkins, Mr. Bruce was put in charge of the Tea nurseries by the Governor-

General, and 20,000 plants and a few Chinamen, Mr. Gordon had brought from China, were sent up to him. Only 8,000 plants were living when they reached their destination, and these were reared was so unskillfully, that not *one* survived ; Mr. Bruce were therefore dependent on the indigenous plant, and was so far successful, that in 1837 he sent to the Tea Committee forty-six chests of Tea ; twelve of these were sent to England, though it was not considered a favorable specimen on account of the difficulties attending the first manufacture, and the length of time it had been exposed to dampness in the transit to Calcutta, still it was pronounced by British brokers as capable of competing with China Tea.

Mr. Bruce, Superintendent of Tea operations, traversed unexplored regions, and discovered large tracts covered with indigenous Tea, and by his knowledge of the language, conciliatory manners, and judicious treatment of the natives, was mainly instrumental in establishing friendly relations with the hill tribes and their chiefs, through whom forests and waste lands were subsequently placed at the disposal of Government.

The Tea manufactured from the indigenous plant was so favorably received, that an offer was made to contract for 1,000 chests at an average of 1*s.* 10½*d.*

to 2*s.* per ℔. The result of this success promising a rich harvest in the future, was the formation of two Companies, one in England and one in Calcutta; these subsequently amalgamated under the name of the Assam Tea Company which is still the largest among the numerous Companies that have since sprung into existence.

Mr. J. Masters, the first gentleman sent up to superintend their operations, fixed his head-quarters in Nazerah, on the banks of the Dikho, seventeen miles south of the sudder station Sibsagar, where it still remains.

Lord Auckland authorised the transfer of two-thirds of the Government plantations, comprising 70,000 acres to the Assam Company, and Mr. Bruce was permitted to join the Company. In 1840 the Assam Company produced 300 chests of Tea, and the Government factories 200.

Captain Veitch prevailed on a Singpho chief to cultivate a garden at one of their villages, which was quite successful.

The first few years of the Assam Company's operations were disappointing; mismanagement reduced it to the verge of bankruptcy; this, however, was averted by the judicious efforts of Messrs. Burkinyoung and Roberts, in rectifying mistakes and the extravagant management of the Company.

The experimental gardens of Government were worked till 1849, when they were sold to a Chinaman for the small sum of Rs. 900, who resold it for half the amount, finally becoming the property of a wealthy London firm.

Tea planters, however, like others, must "live and earn," and profit by the failures as well as the successes that befall, and the Assam Company so far recovered from its depressed condition as to declare a dividend in 1852 on a crop of 267,000 lbs.

The first *private* garden was commenced by Col. Hanny, near Debrughur, and in 1853, there were six in the Lukhimpore, and three in the Sibsagar district; none had been started in the other districts.

The price of Tea rose in England, and applicants for waste land multiplied; Government grant rules were most liberal, forest lands were rent free for twenty years, high grass tracts rent free for ten years, one-fourth of the area rent free *for ever*. In 1862 there were 71,218 acres appropriated to Tea cultivation, 18,322 actually under Tea, and the crop estimated at 1,788,737 lbs. In 1865, according to the official report of Colonel Hopkinson, Commissioner of Assam, there were 366 Tea estates, nineteen of which belonged to Limited Companies, including 499 gardens; the extent of land in lease or rent paying "pottah" was 516,475 acres; the estimated outturn of Tea, 3,226,756 lbs. The imported men, women and children employed numbered 36,258.

Tea planting at this time was in a state of great prosperity, Assam was an "Eldorado," speculation ran high, to possess a Tea estate became a mania, and almost fabulous prices were paid for gardens that had only just been started, and even for waste land. Government began to look sharply for its share of the spoils, and new rules were made fixing the lowest rate of waste land at rupees 2-8 an acre.

Soon afterwards, none was allowed to be sold, except at auction, and competition often ran the prices up to Rs. 20 or 30, even to Rs. 40 an acre for dense jungle which the axe or hoe had never touched. Natives came forward as brisk competitors with these interlopers of their native soil, not generally with the idea of cultivation, but simply for speculation.

The early planters who got their estates for the asking, were enriched by this wild speculation; to them, these were the halcyon days when the ordinary profits of a Tea factory were from fifty to one hundred per cent. when Tea was sold at an average of 2*s.* or 2*s.* 3*d.* per lb., when a young man, after a few years of successful Tea planting, could sell out and return home "for good" on the sunny side of an ample fortune: others with small expenditure would open out a few acres with seedlings, forming part of a large tract of waste land, then become a shareholder in a Company at immense pecuniary profit.

The river steamers had every cabin full of gentlemen in search of a Tea garden for themselves, or some friend ; and young men from England or Scotland, often brothers or relatives of Tea proprietors, were sent to take charge of Tea gardens, eager for the high salaries offered compared with anything they could do at home, but often with a fitness for nothing except to bring disaster on the proprietors.

From 1866 to 1867 there was an increase of cultivation in Assam of 5,000 acres, in the produce of Tea, of 375,000 lbs., and 9,600 laborers were imported into the province.

Tea interests, however, could not endure such reckless speculation, and a general collapse followed, a crushing of high hopes ; many lost heavily, some their *all* ; factories were closed and young men were turned adrift to beg their passage out of the country. Those who had managed prudently were able to tide over the downward current, and have prospered.

An interest that could outlive the severe strain put on Tea cultivation at this time, has a guarantee of becoming a source of individual and national wealth.

Its steady growth and prosperity, since 1869,

place it beyond a doubt that China and Japan will never again monopolize the Tea trade of the world.

Government have profited immensely by the growth of Tea cultivation in the province, but every planter knows by painful experience how slow Government have been in helping them out of their difficulties, or in taking the necessary steps to aid the enterprise ; the most important necessity, good roads and bridges have been, and are still, sadly neglected; some planters during the rainy season for months are completely isolated from the outside world, for want of even a riding path through the jungle, or any means of crossing a deep river ; they cannot see a neighbouring planter, a few miles away. Many restrictions and heavy burdens of expense have been laid upon the planters by numerous laws in regard to land tenure, and cooly emigration, though probably intended to be humane and just.

The whole country is virtually owned by the British Government; a ryot has no claim on the land he has reclaimed from the jungle, or his home, except he receives annually a pottah,—a stamped paper which contains permission to occupy on condition that he pays a fixed amount, Government holding the right at any time to cancel the pottah refuse him the right of occupancy.

A tea planter who requires hundreds or thousands of acres, can obtain them in either of two ways, by what is termed "fee simple,"—the land is bought from Government at a fixed rate per acre, or he can hold land on a perpetual lease, or for thirty years, paying a rent annually at Government rates; *viz.*, the first three years it is free of rent, the fourth year a low rate is required, the fifth year an increased rate, and the sixth year to the end of the lease, the full rate of pottah land.

There has been a decided lull in applications for tea land within the past few years; some say, "the *best* tea land has been secured, but as tea is found to thrive well in almost any soil above inundation, there must still remain vast tracts of rich virgin soil inviting enterprise. Tea is indigenous on the Naga hills, as yet scarcely approached. In the plains, thousands of acres covered with coarse grass, twelve to fifteen feet high, now the lairs of wild beasts, might easily be converted into tea gardens, by being burnt over; such soil has been proved to be favourable for Tea.

The *best* soil is a yellow, light, sandy loam, on rolling land, that readily drains any excess of water. Forest land is better than grass land; low tracts require to be heavily drained, otherwise in the rainy season water standing round them destroys the plants. In the early years of tea planting, grand forests were ruthlessly destroyed, some planters clearing every tree, others leaving here and there one too tall to shade the plants; no prohibition of Government to the cutting of timber existed till 1860; since that time Forest Department officers attend to the preservation of all valuable timber. There are numbers of "reserved forests" containing thousands of trees which are carefully guarded by stringent regulations. A forest officer is located in each sudder station, and a round price levied on every good tree cut for any purpose.

The Tea plant growing wild is from ten to thirty feet in height with a girth of from fifteen to twenty-four inches. In cultivation it is kept pruned to an average of thirty inches.

Tea, botanically, is a species of Camellia, a Polyandrus plant of the order *Ternstiomeca.* It is a hardy evergreen, growing readily from the equator to the forty-fifth degree of latitude. The flowers are white about the size of a wild rose, with single petals; they open in spring and the seed are gathered in October and November. The sale of seed forms no insignificant item of income to the planter, the price varying with the kind of seed, and the demand; the seed of indigenous plants is often as high as two hundred and even three hundred rupees a maund (80 lbs.), one hundred and fifty may be considered an average; Hybrid seed is from fifty to eighty rupees a maund.

The Assam Company in 1882 report seed sold to the amount of £6,599 ; another large estate the same year, from indigenous plants, realized Rs. 75,000 for the sale of seed alone. For the China variety there is no sale of late years.

In the gardens *three* kinds of plants are seen, the Assam, Hybrid, and China. The Hybrid is a cross between the other two, resulting from mingled cultivation. The China plant is not in favor, the other two are found to yield more abundantly, and the leaves are more easily manipulated and have a stronger flavor.

The seeds are planted in nurseries six to eight inches apart, and two inches deep ; this is done in the cold season, and weather and soil being favourable, the seedlings are ready for planting in a year or less.

They are planted in a cleared area 4 × 4 or 5 × 5, and kept carefully hoed and pruned till the third year, when the new shoots are plucked for manufacture.

In the cold season, though the plant keeps quite green, it is comparatively dormant, but about the end of February the sap again flows upward and new shoots are thrown out ; only these are plucked for manufacture. During the dormant season, the bush is pruned to about two and half feet high, and to the shape most conducive to producing a large quantity of leaf.

The top is levelled to a tabular form to present a broad surface of new shoots ; a good Assam Tea bush often measures across the top six to eight feet.

Three years old plants are expected to yield 80lbs. of Tea to the acre, the fourth year twice that amount, in the sixth or seventh year, when it reaches maturity, the yield is from 500 to 800 pounds per acre. The bushes go on yielding at the same rate for twenty years or more, when it begins to lessen. Worn out plants are made to renew their youth by being pruned down to within a few inches of the ground. The average yield of a Tea bush is one pound of leaf, or four ounces of manufactured Tea. This may seem small, but it must be borne in mind that there are from two to three thousand plants on an acre.

The average yield of Tea gardens in *all* India, is given as 256 lbs. per acre, of Assam *alone* 280 lbs.

The leaf is plucked as often as the bushes "flush," that is, throw out new shoots, which ordinarily occurs every ten or fifteen days, from the first of March till the middle of November ; the remainder of the year the plant rests.

A Tea garden in full bearing, clean and well kept, with its regular rows of bright green stretching off in the distance without interruption over hundreds of acres of waving land, is one of the most beautiful sights in the world.

TEA MANUFACTURE.

CHAPTER XI.

TEA, in the home market, is sold under the various names of Hyson, Ulong, Pekoe, Souchong, Congou, &c.; these names by some may be supposed to indicate a different plant, but the difference solely depends on different soil and climate, and different modes of manufacture in China, Japan, or India.

The new soft shoots *only* are plucked, consisting of a leaf bud, glistening with a silvery down, and two leaves; the third leaf is plucked, if new and soft, but not the stalk; the axil is left from which a new shoot will come.

Plucking is mostly done by women and children in groups, each one with a deep basket hung on the shoulder. The "nirik," or task required, is eight seers (16 lbs.) of leaf a day from a woman, and four seers from a child; many do more than this, and some bring in a maund of leaf in a day; to encourage plucking a higher rate is allowed on the excess of the "nirik"; this is one pice a seer, for the excess one and a half, or two pice are paid, each plucker's load is weighed when brought in, and the leaf at once spread on mats or wicker pans to wither over night. In the morning if on account of the cool temperature it is not perfectly placid, it is rendered so by being spread in the sun, then it is ready for rolling. This was done entirely by hand, till a few years ago machines were invented by Kinmond and Jackson, Assam planters, to perform this work more expeditiously.

For hand-rolling, a man took a heap of the withered leaf on a rough bamboo mat, and rolled it back and forth in a ball shape under his hands, turning it over and shaking it out light, now and again, rolling till the leaf had a curled appearance, and so wet with the juice it can easily be pressed into a heap for fermentation. Hand-rolling is still the mode of manufacture in China and Japan, but in India, the rolling machine has quite supplanted hand labor, the machine doing the work more effectively, cleaner, quicker, and saving labor, which is an important consideration in a country where labor is so scarce.

The machine is run by a steam engine and rolls a maund of leaf in about twenty minutes; the engine at the same time is frequently made to run a sifting and fanning machine. During the machine-rolling process the juice exudes and converts it into a wet mass, which is left to ferment; when this is complete the leaf has become a dark reddish brown, and gives out a strong aroma.

It is now ready for drying, and for this purpose it is spread lightly over wicker trays an inch or two thick, and placed over a charcoal fire made in a shallow cavity in the ground. The rest for the tray is basket work plastered, or brick work about three feet high. The tray is frequently removed, and the Tea turned that it may dry evenly, and great care is necessary lest it remain too long, and the leaf acquires a burnt flavor.

The custom, after hand-rolling, is to throw the leaf into a hot iron pan, turning it briskly with a stiff brush, then rolling and panning again before drying ; this slow process, taught by Chinese manufacturers in Assam, has passed away. When the leaf is thoroughly dry, it is cooled and put into large bins.

Before packing, it is sorted through sieves of different degrees of fineness ; the finest giving the Flowery Pekoe, which is the leaf bud with a silvery sheen, the next Pekoe, Pekoe Souchong and Souchong ; the remainder is made into Broken Tea, and Dust Tea.

After sorting, the Tea is fanned on a bamboo pan by hand, or by machinery, then carefully picked by women and children of stems and other superfluous matter.

Formerly what was termed "red leaf," that is, leaf too hard for proper manipulation, was thrown away by tons, now, however, a more economical plan is in vogue; this leaf is broken fine by machinery and sent to market as Broken Tea.

Each sort of tea is bulked in sufficient quantity to form an even break. Before packing, it is dried over a slow charcoal fire for some hours, and packed while warm in boxes lined with lead, soldered air tight, and marked when it is ready for shipment. Each box is marked with the kind of tea it contains and with initials indicating the estate.

The process of manufacture here described is for *Black Tea* alone, the only tea produced in Assam.

A tea factory is a busy place. A glance inside will show you a rolling machine in motion and another sorting tea, a dozen trays sliding back and forth doing the work of as many men; in another place a group of women, each with a big pan of tea before her, and a naked, fat, rollicking baby on the ground beside her. No machinery can do the women's work in picking tea. Green tea, is largely manufactured at the gardens on the Himalayas; the chief difference in the process being, that the leaf is put at once into hot pans, without withering, and after being rolled in a circular motion, it is dried quickly in hot pans, then sorted into the different varieties known as Gun powder, Hyson, etc.

In Japan, the process of coloring tea is thus described. " After the leaf has been through the hot pan four or five pounds are taken and thrown into pans heated to a temperature of 212 Farhenheit, and rapidly stirred by hand against the smooth iron surface about twenty minutes, then a teaspoonful of thoroughly pulverized soapstone (saponite) and five grains of powdered Chinese indigo are thoroughly rubbed into the leaf some twenty minutes; then half a teaspoonful of gypsum, and of pulverized tamarack (a species of larch) is added and the stirring and rubbing continued for some time; it is then put into cold pans and cold rubbed against the iron, till it has acquired a polish, which is arrived at in about an hour." These ingredients may not be especially injurious; doubtless they are less so than those used in China, where Prussian Blue is said to be used for manufacturing green teas, and Black lead for Black teas, with other ingredients dangerous to health, still who would not prefer the pure, simple, *unadultreated uncoloured* Assam tea?

The manufacture of "Brick Tea" sold on the northern frontier is a secret of the northern tribes; each brick weighs four pounds, and they are in demand at the high price of eight shillings per pound.

The estimate of expenses in the manufacture of tea is variously given, much depending on the skill of the planter in managing economically. Proprietors generally manage their gardens, for obvious reasons more economically than employés. Tea Companies usually employ one general Manager, on a salary of from 300 to 600 Rs. a month, and for the several gardens an Assistant, on salaries ranging from 50 to 250 Rs. per month. The perquisites of these situations are a house free of rent, an elephant or pony, and two or three servants. Where machinery is used an engineer is employed, and in every factory establishment, a carpenter, blacksmith and several native overseers are employed.

The law requires that all persons employed be provided with houses, and medical attendance; in large Companies a European doctor is employed, but usually a Bengallee doctor, educated and diplomaed in a Calcutta college, attends to the sick among the laborers, medicines being supplied by the propriotors.

There is usually a large comfortable bungalow for the Superintendent and, now-a-days, a fire-proof building for the Tea-house. Near by, are rows of huts built separately, side by side, for coolies. If there are different tribes, Bengallees and Cacharees, there are separate rows of huts, as these people never minglo. Cooly wages are five or six rupees a month. Much of the hoeing and plucking is done as task work.

In opening out a new garden, there is considerable outlay in buildings for the establishment, and every year, some expenses of this kind. The expenses of the first clearance with the necessary buildings, irrespective of the price of the land, is estimated at an average of Rs. 80 an acre; for the second and third year Rs. 70. The plant now begins to yield a crop of 80 lbs. to the acre, the fourth year 160 lbs., the fifth year 240 lbs., the sixth year when in full bearing from 300 to 500 lbs. of manufactured Tea.

"* Assuming the cost to be per acre £7, the following table will give the actual cost of producing and selling an average crop of four maunds, 320 lbs. per acre.

1.	Superintendence and cultivation per acre	£7 on 320 lbs. £0-0-5¼
2.	Plucking 13*s.* 3*d.* per maund ...	£0-0-2
3.	Manufacturing 11*s.* 3*d.* per maund ...	£0-0-1⅛
4.	Box and lead 6*s.* 6*d.* per box ...	£0-0-1
5.	Country transport and commission per box 6*s.* 6*d.*	£0-0-1
6.	Freight and home charges per lb. ...	£0-0-2½
	Total cost of cultivation, manufacture and sale per lb.	£0-1-1

Machinery has reduced the expense to 10 or 11 pence per lb.

Again taking £ 7 as the fixed annual charge, and the cost of manufacture and sale at £2-11-7 per maund, the following table will give the cost per lb. according to the rate of production; 80 lbs. per acre £9-11-7 or 2*s.* 4¾*d.* per lb.

* Report of Mr. A. Maurice, Commissioner on Tea cultivation in India.

160 lbs.	... £12- 3-2	or	1*s.*	6½*d*.	per lb.
240 lbs.	... £14-14-9	,,	1*s.*	2¾*d.*	,,
320 lbs.	... £17- 6-4	,,	1*s.*	1*d.*	,,
400 lbs.	... £19-7-11	,,	1*s.*	——	,,

In practice, £20 per acre, which 400 lbs. ought to give, is not counted on from ten to fifteen is the highest profit anticipated." The smallest outturn at which it is estimated tea can be profitably cultivated is three, or three and a half maunds per acre, at a cost of not more than Rs. 40 per maund or 8 annas per lb.

These figures are only an approximate estimate which many circumstances may modify; there is similar uncertainty attending Tea cultivation as in the production of wheat, rice, or other crops; the season may prove unfavorable,—in drought the plant does not flush, in an excess of rain, the leaf is wanting in flavor, if the market is overstocked prices are low; these and other things may lessen produce or lessen profits.

Those who can afford to wait for the returns of the season's crop, usually send their tea direct to England, but far the largest proportion of Assam Tea is sold by agents in Calcutta at auction; some concerns are so pressed for funds, that they draw from the agents advances on the season's crop.

The expense on Tea laid down in Calcutta is one anna a pound, and the additional expense of sending to London about eight annas a pound.

Indian Tea now supplies one-third the consumption of Great Britain, and when we glance over the past quarter century, and remember that the "Flowery kingdom" then had the entire monopoly of the Tea trade, we shall be ready to affirm that Indian Tea cultivation is a grand success. Indian Tea from the outset, has been pronounced superior to China and realized a higher price.

The "Tea Syndicate" is rapidly opening new markets for Indian teas in Australia, the United States, and latterly, on the continent of Europe. In 1882, 682,882 lbs. were sent to the United States. The Assam Company report 2,718,000 lbs. sent to Australia and New Zealand, and 641,000 lbs. to America.

Its superior strength, delicious flavor, and furthermore, the entire freedom from adulteration of Indian tea must bring it into favor with tea drinking people everywhere. Tea merchants are said to mix China with Indian teas to enhance the value of the former, while it cheapens the latter, and in this way its virtues may reach the poorer classes.

Within the memory of the present generation, is the time when Tea was a luxury even among the well-to-do, and rarely tasted by the poor ; gradually it is become almost a necessity in every family, and best of all, in a measure, it is supplanting intoxicating beverages; it is in constantu se probably by one-third of the human race ; its slightly stimulating properties bringing relief to the thirsty, comfort to the sick, and rest to the weary.

The success which has attended Tea culture in India, may be said to have benefitted the *world*, inasmuch as mankind are no longer dependent on a walled and sealed kingdom for one of its greatest comforts, and the gratitude of nations is due to Him from whom cometh every good and perfect gift.

Dry statistics are most uninteresting to some, but there are others who may have an interest in the following figures indicating the growth, and results of this industry in Assam.

Land under Tea in 1874 as reported in Lind's pamphlet—

In the Kamrup district	... ...	4,635 acres.
In the Durrung district	... ...	13,933 ,,
In the Nowgong district	... ...	8,481 ,,
In the Sibsagar district	... ...	34,094 ,,
In the Lukhimpore district	... ...	21,942 ,,
The crop of Tea for 1881 in the Assam valley	... ...	24,390,732 lbs.
The crop of Cachar and Sylhet		13,903,010 ,,

In 1882, 743 gardens in the Assam valley, 247 in the Surma valley : total 990.

Area under cultivation	... ...	178,851 acres.
Total area held ...	... ...	193,362 ,,
Increase in five years	... ...	195,593 ,,
Yield of Tea ...	...	45,472,941 lbs.

Manufactured in the Assam valley	28,098,805	lbs.
Manufactured in the Surma valley	17,383,136	„

Increase 20 per cent. over preceding year.

Average yield per acre ...	... 290	lbs.
Average previous year, per acre ...	... 282	„
Among the Tea districts Cachar leads the list with an outturn of ...	... 12,721,327	lbs.
Sibsagar comes next with ...	... 11,337,437	„
Lukhimpore	... 8,125,257	„
Sylhet	... 4,166,209	„
Kamrup	... 951,354	„
Goalpara	... 66,278	„

Average cost of Cultivation.

In Goalpara Rs. 45 to 50 per acre.
Cost of Tea Manufacture 2½ ans. per ℔.
In Kamrup 30 to 100 Rs. per acre.
Manufacture 5 to 9 ans. per ℔.
In Nowgong 70 Rs. an acre.
Manufacture 7 ans. per ℔.
In Lukhimpore 240 Rs. per acre.
Manufacture from 5 to 8 ans. per ℔.
In Cachar 100 to 120 Rs. per acre.
Manufacture 5 annas per ℔.
In Sylhet, Rs. 59-11-0 per acre.
Manufacture 5 ans. per ℔.

The most prominent features of the season of 1883 is the decline in the average value of the crop, and the large increase of consumption.

THE PLANTER'S LIFE.

CHAPTER XII.

The situation of a Tea Planter is no sinecure, though if we were to judge from the eagerness with which the place is sought, we might think it was. The salary and perquisites invite numerous applicants for every vacancy that occurs, and it is not uncommon to find young men willing to work, and find themselves for a time, in the hope of obtaining a "Billet in Tea."

It is true, the European Planter is a superintendent only, he has none of the actual work on a garden to perform, this would be impossible in the climate of India, besides, this would compromise his dignity in the eyes of the natives, whose crude idea of a gentleman is, one who has plenty of money, and nothing to do, so when "distance lends enchantment to the view" the situation may seem an easy one; while in fact, the difficulties are sufficient to tax the industry, ingenuity, and patience of any one to the utmost.

The laborers are his greatest care, whether contractors, local laborers, or imported coolies.

Clearing land, and making charcoal, are usually

done by Assamese contractors who often prove wholly unreliable ; they are paid advances on the work to secure it being done promptly, but even with this inducement there is often great delay, or the work is not done at all. In this case, they must be prosecuted, which involves a journey of the Planter to the Court of the nearest station, causing expense and loss of time. Local coolies are equally untrustworthy, the planter is so desirous of their work, that he willingly gives advances, perhaps for a month's work, which may be fulfilled in six months, or *never.* Not unlikely the man has taken advances from several, and then scatters his time among them so as to appear to be fulfilling his agreement. There is no limit to the knavery the planter has to deal with.

Imported coolies are frequently running away, others are ill, or pretending to be, some are quarrelsome, or refractory, and *all* are naturally lazy. To each gang of coolies at their work, one man is employed to look after them.

The coolies are a motley company of antagonistic castes and habits, and without great discretion and tact, the Planter cannot manage successfully, and the final success of a garden depends more upon the proper management of the pepole, than any other *one* thing. If their peculiar, and perhaps foolish prejudices are ignored, they will not be content to remain, and their complaints, though often groundless, cannot always be disregarded.

Among a batch of newly arrived coolies, may be observed two tall gaunt men with the "poitre," sacred thread on their shoulders, marking them as Brahmins; they refuse to handle the hoe, it is against their *caste*, they think they would be degraded by such employment, they were *born* to idleness, and to live by the gifts those of lower caste have the *honor* to bestow; such is their lofty view of *themselves*; the planters may show these proud beggars the agreement they made to serve as coolies, but they reply, "We did not understand about it," which is doubtless true, for they cannot read or write, and their ignorance is taken advantage of by cooly contractors. It is utterly useless to contend with a man's *caste* prejudices, and while seeming to gratify them, by tact, the Planter manages to get his money's worth out of the men in the variety of work the garden affords. Unscrupulous cooly contractors send up the lame, halt, and blind fit only for the hospital, and many find a watery grave on the passage up the river.

There is great improvement over the early days of Tea planting, when the steamer decks were crowded with men, women and children, no proper attention given to the sick, and no railing to prevent those sleeping near the edge from rolling off into the river; and many were lost in this way alone. Frequently cholera broke out, and carried them off by scores, regretted, perhaps, by some bereaved relative, and by the Planter on account of his financial loss.

These irregularities were corrected some years since by stringent Government enactments, obliging the steamers to provide a given space for coolies and a firm railing, also to provide nourishing food, warm blankets, and a doctor especially to attend on them ; in consequence there is far less suffering and mortality, though every year cholera finds some victims on the steamers.

During the cold season, nearly every steamer brings up from two to five hundred emigrants for the Tea gardens ; they come from Bengal, Sontal, Chota Nagpore, and other thickly settled districts. A three years agreement has been the rule, now five years are required.

The garden work is of sufficient capacity to allow different nationalities, generally, being employed by themselves. In looking after all the details of the work, where hundreds of coolies are employed, there is evidently enough to keep a Planter busy ; he usually rises early, and after a *chota hazree*—little breakfast of tea and toast—he spends from three to five hours in a walk or ride over the plantation, inspecting the work and giving general directions to the *mohorís* (overseers.) These *mohorís* are often knavish and exacting ; give a native power and he is likely to be tyrannical, as native history proves. Coolies are often cheated out of a portion of their wages, and to prevent fraud, planters often oblige the *mohorí* to pay the hands in their presence, or what is better, pay them personally. Even this does not always prevent cheating ; in cunning and deceit the native can outwit his English master ; this characteristic of the people is a perpetual source of irritation, and it requires firm control and a good temper to get on comfortably.

Sickness among the laborers is less a source of anxiety than formerly, since Government require every garden to employ a doctor, and provide medicines. Fever and bowel complaints prevail at all seasons ; cases of cholera among new arrivals are frequent ; with the best care, loss of coolies by death or runaway is often occurring, and from these two causes alone, *twenty-five per cent.* of the whole number of coolies on a garden has been known to be lost, though this case was an extreme one.

On many plantations, it has been a constant care to keep the numerous laborers supplied with food ; the local market being insufficient, hundreds of maunds of rice are constantly being brought up on the steamers for the gardens, besides dhal, salt and oil, the essentials of native diet. A Government regulation obliges the Planter to supply the rice at a fixed rate, whatever may be the market price; this sometimes subjects them to great loss; in addition to the high rates for freight on the steamer, the grain must often be taken a long journey on bullock carts from the landing to the garden.

The importation of so numerous a foreign population is working many changes, *one* that every one feels is the rise in the price of food-supplies, in fact, a difficulty is experienced in getting some things at any price; another yearly increasing difficulty is that of labor; wages have doubled, and in some places quadrupled, and in the rainy season, it is next to impossible to get half a dozen coolies on *any* terms. Even Government officers have great difficulty in getting Government work done, they are obliged to put the screws of force on, through a Mozedah. Of late they are employing convicts on roads and bridges.

The Tea Planter's domestic and social life is not of an enviable kind, especially if he is a bachelor, which is usually the case; he has few opportunities for sociability, his occupation makes him "Monarch of all he surveys" for miles around, and his *nearest* neighbours are several miles distant; his bungalow, as

European houses are called, though the largest at the garden, is often a rough affair, built of the product of the jungle, just at hand, and if far from any station he has few comforts to smooth his rough home, and contents himself to live in a camp style, only too glad when friends come to offer them "a shake down," and to provide his *best*, for the Planter is generously hospitable.

Rice and fowls are the staples of his monotonous meals the year round, the "lines have fallen to him in pleasant places" if he can get a supply of milk, eggs, and bread; instead of the "staff of life," he substitutes "chapatees;" for the uninitiated, we will explain, that these are very thin cakes, made of flour and water, baked on an iron pan over the fire; it is the unleavened bread of ancient times, still very common in India.

There are exceptions, of course, to the style of living described, of late there has been great improvement in the bungalows built, now many, and specially in the Assam Company have large brick houses, and those near stations live in comfortable style. Planters, generally, are good horseman and sportsman, and often supply their tables with the luxuries of game-pigeon, snipe, and wild fowl, with an occasional dish of venison; the canned provisions, now sent all over the world give variety to his table fare. It is no unusual thing for the Royal Bengal tiger to prowl about his dwelling by night, and carry off unprotected man, or beast; fortunately, the savage beast does not know his power, or often the frail wall that only *hides* his prey would be but paper in his fierce claws. The ornaments of the Planter's house are the trophies won on his *private* battle field. Insects in nameless variety swarm around his lamp in the evening, and mosquitoes, and in some places, gnats, are such pests day and night, that there is no escape except under a mosquito curtain. Venomous snakes may ensconce themselves in a corner of his bungalow, or stretch their length from the thatch roof above him; from ants, the universal household pest, he cannot hope to escape; to keep clear of rats and mice, some planters have half a dozen cats. In many cases, the comforts that a planter might enjoy have been ignored in the haste to get rich; every man's work *tells* on the garden, and it cannot be spared to add to his comfort. Proprietors especially have no idea of remaining longer than is necessary to make a garden that will sell at a large profit, or yield a comfortable income, and every consideration, not essential to this single purpose, must give way.

As every garden includes a large tract of country, planters are necessarily in an isolated stuation, and this means great loneliness, some for weeks, and in some cases, in the rainy season, for months, do not see a person to speak to, in their own language; in the cold season the roads and bridges may admit of a planter riding a pony to his neighbouring planters, or to the station. Planters have done much, without Government aid, to open communication with each other. In 1865 Government granted forty lacs (40,00000) of Rupees to construct a trunk road from Dhubri to Sadiya, but the "Grand Trunk Road" in many parts is still a myth, and much more needs to be done to render travelling comfortable.

Most planters temper their loneliness with numerous pet animals, dogs, cats, birds, monkeys, &c., they are fortunate if they are musical, and can make an instrument enliven their home, or artistical, and can while away a weary hour in transferring to canvass the rare scenes of beauty to be found in Assam; but the *one* thing a planter most needs is a *wife and family*, they are the safeguards of virtue, happiness, and success; rarely does the married man fall into the excesses which are common with bachelors; besides, the latter is in a pitiable condition when sickness lays him low, and he has no friend near, but must depend on ignorant and careless servants; there may be no physician within many miles except his cooly doctor, with whom he fears to trust his case. Planters have sickened and died under just such circumstances.

Fever is the most prevalent disease. Newly opened gardens are especially malarious, comparatively few however, have died, some have been forced to leave, others by taking a trip on the river, return to enjoy many years of good health. Liver complaint is not uncommon among Europeans, but with temperate habits and proper attention to unnecessary exposure, health is as likely to be enjoyed in Assam as anywhere else.

A Planter's greatest danger lies in the influence of his surroundings ; he may have left the protecting roof of a father, the yearning influence of a mother's love, the chaste and purifying companionship of a sister ; the high moral tone of the home circle is far away, and the sacred influence of the Sabbath ; he finds himself as free as the monkeys chattering among the trees to *do as he pleases,* restraint is gone, there is no one to notice his conduct for whom he cares "a rap," and the danger is, he will ignore his knowledge of an All-seeing Eye, and sink into habits he would blush to own ; young men who can bravely meet the difficulties and endure the discomforts incident to the work, often prove wanting in the *moral* courage necessary to resist the temptations that assail their peculiar situation.

Not a few young men who come to the country, noble specimens of upright manhood, have under the circumstances described, become in a few years perfect wrecks.

The first danger is the habit of taking "pegs," then the gaming table, and kindred vices follow; step by step and unconsciously to himself, the man's virtue and manliness are in the dust. The situation is a fiery ordeal which none but a firm Christian character can endure unscorched.

The sons of Great Britian, who mostly compose the Europeans of Assam, as yet have scarcely felt the tide of temperance which has flowed over the republic of America, and converted thousands of homes to the total abstinence principle.

The custom that prevails here of offering a caller a "peg," and the sentiment that it would not be polite to do otherwise, was the case in America a half century ago, but which has now entirely passed away; drinking "pegs," slings, "cocktails" and other decoctions of liquor, is now confined to Bar-rooms and in one state, Kansas, *these* places are prohibited. The idea that liquor is necessary to health is a serious mistake; experience has proved that the most temperate enjoy the best health and live the longest as a general rule. No disease induced by the climate is a tenth part so fatal as the habit of drinking liquor. Baron Leibeg, the famous chemist, has proved to a certainty, "that as much flour as can lie on the point of a knife, is more nutritious than eight quarts of Bavarian Beer, counted the *best*, and that there is as much nutriment in a five pound loaf of bread, or three pounds of flesh, as in 730 gallons of beer." This is not the opinion of an enthusiastic temperance man, but of one of the ablest chemists in Europe.

"Why spend your money for that which is not bread, and your labor for that which satisfieth not?" Why not find sufficient stimulant in the cup that cheers but not inebriates? With the *best tea in the world* at hand, let the time hasten when the Planter of Assam will so far follow the example of his coadjutors in the "Flowery kingdom," as tomake a cup of tea a token of hospitality instead of a "peg."

Any resident of Assam must observe that there has been of late years a marked improvement in Planter society, there is more sobriety and steady application to work, and more general observance of the Sabbath in suspending unnecessary work; the clergyman is welcomed to hold services in many gardens, and especially, that there has been a yearly increase in the number of married planters, four-fold probably, within five years, which has a decided purifying influence. Married ladies frequently bring an unmarried sister, or friend with them for society in their isolated home, which usually results in another marriage, and is a matter for congratulation where ladies are so few, for every one will admit, that pure exalted womanhood raises the moral tone of society.

We do not intend to leave the impression that the Tea Planter is any more given to an erratic course than most young men under similar circumstances, but that the circumstances are especially a severe test of moral character.

Among them are fine musicians, artists and scientists; few ever go beyond the bounds of moderate drinking, and it is to be hoped when temperance principles are more generally adopted, and married planters are the *rule* not the *exception*, as at present, that Assam will be truly styled "The happy valley."

ANIMALS.

CHAPTER XIII.

The sound that especially arrests the attention of a newcomer to India is the "Caw-caw" of a multitude of crows; it is the first greeting of dawn and at sundown the settlement of a flock for the night, is preceded by a general conference in Caw-caw language; it is amusing to watch them. A group settle on the ground close together, one says, "Caw-caw," another "Caw-caw," responses go round, one here and there hops a few paces, bob their heads, cock one eye to the speaker, then the other, the company varying the manœuvres till a decision seems to be reached by a vote of the majority, then all fly off together to a tree top for the night.

To the house-keeper, crows are a pest, nothing eatable escapes their searching eyes, nothing unprotected, their ravenous maw; a servant in passing from cook-house to bungalow is liable to lose the contents of his dish, or they boldly fly into the house and snatch food from the table.

Their movements are often very amusing and show remarkable cunningness; when one gets a titbit he selfishly wishes to enjoy alone, he carefully hides it from his fellows under the leaves on the ground, or in the roof thatch. Their cunningness is illustrated in this *true* story. "Three crows were watching a dog eat a piece of meat and tried to snatch it, but in vain; they flew off a short distance and seemed to have contrived a plan; they flew back and two went as near as they dared to the meat, while the third crow gave the dog's tail a sharp bite; of course, he turned with a yelp, when the two seized the meat, flew away, and the three shared it."

On the whole, we must acknowledge the crow a useful bird; one of the Creator's gifts for removing what would breed disease in a hot climate.

Hawks and vultures serve a similar good purpose, but are comparatively few, "wheresoever the carcass is there you may see them gathered together."

In this brief glimpse, it is impossible to notice particularly the great variety of birds in Assam; there are many with beautiful plumage, but there are few sweet singers; a chirp, a whistle, or a double note, is the most we usually hear from forest birds.

Game is plentiful, wild fowls are found in coveys, also two species of pheasant and peacock; the black variety, in coveys of from ten to fifty; these are snared by the Assamese, and brought for sale. Partridges, quails, jacksnipe, pigeons, and parrots are very numerous.

Two varieties of wild geese come to the plains in the cold season, and ducks and other water-fowl are plentiful on the ponds and streams.

The owl's dismal hoot often breaks the still hours of the night; one large species has a frightful cry of "Hudu! Hudu! Dudu," in a voice so human, that one wakes from a dream of some one in agony.

Flying foxes frequent high trees, and at night devour any fruit they can find. A small bat is troublesome, habiting under a thatch roof, and often flying about the house at night.

The worst night disturbers in Assam are the numerous jackals; the sun has scarcely set when they emerge from their hiding-places in packs; one begins with a loud "yow! yowoo!" another joins in the cry, then the whole pack, as they run along, howl, scream, screech, yelp, and whine, making a jumble of hideous noises, that can be heard a long distance. Just before dawn, when one is taking their soundest sleep, is a favourite time for a jackal concert; they seem to be calling all their fellows to a feast on the fowls or ducks on your premises that may not be very strongly secured.

There are night visitors of a stronger and more dangerous kind; your cattle and horses are not safe when a leopard or tiger is prowling about your dwelling, which is not an unusual occurrence, as every

ASIATIC TIGER.

one knows who has been many months in Assams Even the stations are not exempt from frequent visits. from these denizens of the jungle; there are always tracts of jungle near where they lie concealed in the day time, and they often spring out, and carry off cattle that are straying near, even in sight of the herdsman. In more than one station we have known a tiger to prowl about the house in the night; in one instance, he boldly jumped a fence with a calf in his mouth, and quietly devoured it at the back of the cook-house where the bones were found in the morning. Nearly every night in the cold season the cry of "peu, peu," may be heard indicating the proximity of the hungry beast; the cry is said to be that of an animal that always precedes the tiger, some say a jackal, but what animal, it is we cannot say, but we know the tiger is near when we hear that cry.

To diminish their number, Government give a bounty of rupees twenty-five for every fresh skin, with head attached, brought to the Court, and in every station natives are frequent recipients, still there seems to be no diminution in their numbers, nor is there likely to be while so large a portion of the country affords a safe hiding-place for them.

Officers, planters, and natives find most exciting sport in hunting them. It is a dangerous sport, though seated inside a "howdah" on the back of a trained elephant, and many can tell a tale of narrow escapes, while occasionally, life is sacrificed. A wounded tiger will sometimes fiercely attack an elephant; at one time when this occurred, the elephant shook himself with such violence, that he threw a gentleman out of the "howdah" to the ground on one side of him, while the tiger fell on the other; fortunately, not observing the fallen man, he made off; many equally narrow escapes might be related: we will indulge, however, only in one story of a tiger hunt. Two gentlemen were out hunting, when, spotting a tiger, they followed him up till within range of their guns, when they fired and wounded the beast in the chest, with a loud roar, he bounded off, the elephant following, till they saw him in open ground about thirty yards distance; they now dismounted and cautiously aiming, fired again, the charge entering the stomach, but he ran off into a paddy field. The elephant was sent in to hunt him out, when the tiger sprang upon him, and he took fright and bolted. The tiger lay down in the field, and the gentlemen again fired; just as they did so, he opened his mouth, and the charge entered his jaws; he was now only about ten yards distant, and one of the sportsman saw the beast fix his eyes upon him, and with a savage roar he sprung towards him; the gentleman attempted to climb a tree, but had raised himself only about four feet from the ground, when the tiger sprang upon him, bringing him to the ground on one side the tree, while the tiger fell back on the other with half his clothes in his mouth, which he had wrenched off, leaving his victims back well scored with his sharp claws. For a second the clothes in the brute's mouth took his attention, which his victim improved to scramble up and make off with all possible speed; the tiger followed some distance, but finally left him. All this time the other sportsman was up a tree, a helpless spectator of the exciting scene, having thrown his gun on the ground in his haste to escape. Again they mounted the elephant and went in search of the tiger, being sure the wounds were mortal; they found him dead, having bled to death from the mouth wound. They hung the carcass on the elephant, and bore off their hard earned trophy.

In travelling we occasionally come upon traces of a deserted village, and on inquiring the cause, are told a man-eating tiger prowled about and carried off some of the people. A man-eater at one time infested one of the public roads in the Sibsagar district, and for twelve days every day one man was seized while passing on the road; several travelling together did not intimidate the beast; at last, a native climbed a tree near his haunt and watched; some men were heard coming on the road,—the tiger slyly crept out to seize his prey, when a shot from the man on the tree entered his breast, and he dropped dead. The man was rewarded double the usual bounty for his brave and beneficent act.

Tigers are said to be man-eaters only when from age they have lost most of their teeth and claws and have thus lost the power to seize their usual prey.

Mrs. C., the wife of a missionary, gives a graphic description of a tiger hunt in the Naga hills.

The village had for some time been molested with the depredations of a tiger on the cattle, and latterly on men. One day, where land was clearing for a rice crop, a woman who was gathering firewood suddenly disappeared; men working near heard a suppressed scream, and rustling of the jungle, and suspected at once the terrible fate of their companion, and fleeing to the village, they got men with guns to return in pursuit, but darkness soon obliged them to abandon it. The next day, the whole village turned out for a real tiger hunt. Their custom is to surround a large piece of jungle, in which the tiger is supposed to be lurking, build a stockade on the lower side of the hill, and fill the ground just above it with long "pongees"—sharpened pieces of bamboo which piercing, inflict dangerous wounds; when all is ready, the Nagas, bound to stand by each other for life or death, start *en masse* from the upper side armed only with spears and knife-like hatchets ; with cutting and slashing, with whoops and yells, they beat downward, hoping to frighten the beast on to the "pongees," when he is quickly despatched. In the present instance, the remains of the woman being early found, it was decided to abandon the hunt and poison the corpse, as a surer way of killing the tiger, for the habit of the animal is to return to its unconsumed prey.

Repugnant as this abuse of the human form was, for the sake of the living, a large quantity of strychnine was injected into the corpse, and there left.

The third day after, a man-eating tiger, a huge creature, was stretched lifeless near his victim, himself a victim to his own cruelty. On beholding him such shouts, yells, and hurrahs went up from these children of the forest ! They were not satisfied, till they had borne the carcass in triumph up to their village, where again, the air was rent with their loud hurrahs.

The leopard, called, "Putika Bâg," spotted tiger or "Lota Bâg," climbing tiger, is often seen in travelling or hunting, and is a frequent night visitor about the stations, making game of calves, goats and dogs.

Wild buffaloes are numerous and dangerous animals to encounter, especially as olitary bull, with a large pair of sharp horns measuring from tip to tip from eight to twelve feet. Herds are often seen on the banks of the Brahmaputra; passengers on the steamers amuse themselves by shooting them, and the huge alligators that lie stretched on the sand banks. Large herds of tame buffaloes graze on the "churs" formed by the changing river current; these are kept for their milk, which is much richer than cow's milk; a large quantity is converted into ghee, clarified butter,—an article universally used in India for culinary purposes, both by Europeans and natives.

Deer of several species roam over the plains, and antelopes are found near the northern hills. Porcupines are numerous, and strange to say,—a Hindu, who never eats the flesh of other animals, does not object to the porcupine; even a Brahmin, does not count it unclean. The "Bonrou," a burrowing animal, resembling the armadilla, is equally esteemed.

The forests abound in different species of monkeys, a small grey kind are the most numerous; there are also long-armed, black-faced baboons, and two kinds of Gibbon apes, whose loud cry "Hulu" can be heard miles distant; also a rarer kind, a small pretty white monkey with a pink face.

There are two species of wild dogs, a large kind that hunt in pairs, sufficiently strong to kill a horse or deer; and a small kind that hunt in packs.

There are three species of wild cats, one marked

Professor "Smutt" on the Kurai

like a tiger, another like a leopard, and a grey one, that often makes havoc in a fowl house at night.

The wild boar is a formidable beast and not uncommon near the hills ; their tusks are highly prized as an ornament by the Nagas.

The black bear, bison or Mithun, and the rhinoceros are often shot or captured near the hills.

before they are let out to graze the fore feet are chained together, lest they should run away and be lost. Almost every thing that grows is fodder for them; coarse high grass, reeds, bushes, and branches of trees, which they snap off with the greatest ease. When the mahout brings them in for the night, he compels them to load their backs with fodder: long jungle grass, palm leaves, plantain trees, and tree branches are piled up and hanging to the ground on each side; he comes in, an amusing sight,–a high heap of walking jungle; however huge the load, it all disappears before morning in the queer pointed aperture under the foot of his trunk.

Elephants have a convenient water stomach for a hot country; when crossing a river they stop and draw the water into their trunks, then throw it down their throats many times till satisfied; when heated, they draw it out again and give themselves a shower bath, which may not be quite as agreeable to their riders as themselves.

Elephants, in their wild state, are very long lived, judging from dentition and other circumstances; they are supposed to live from one hundred and fifty to two hundred years. It is reported that the remains of a dead *wild* elephant has never been seen by those who have travelled extensively through elephant jungle. Among the people there is a belief that they never die ; others say that when they feel the approach of dissolution, they go to some place unseen by any one to end their days.

When domesticated, they are not as hardy and enduring as we would suppose from their size and strength ; great care is needed not to overwork them as they easily fall ill, and die from want of regular food and rest. The Assam species has a high ridged backbone which is apt to be chafed by any heavy burden ; to prevent this a wadded pad, called a "guddee" is fastened across the back when used either for burdens or riding. They soon know their keepers, and are wonderfully docile and obedient ; the "subjection of every beast of the field" to man at the creation, is strikingly exemplified in the elephant ; if he was conscious of his strength in comparison with his master's, he could never be tamed. The driver uses an ugly weapon, a short pointed iron rod with a hook on one side ; if the beast does not behave properly, he strikes the rod into the top of his head or ears, the blow often bringing blood, and a loud scream from the angry beast.

They are said rarely to breed in captivity, their numbers must therefore be replenished by capture, and the jungles of Assam are a prolific source of supply; Government annually sell at auction the Keddahs" in the different districts ; in addition to the auction price, which is always large, Government have claimed a right of pre-emption of every elephant captured between six and seven and a half feet in height, and a royalty of Rs. 100 on every elephant not purchased by Government. The pre-emption claim has recently been removed.

The "Keddahs" surround salt springs where the herds congregate to drink ; a strong palisade of the trunks of small trees, set close together, is built around a large enclosure ; at the farthest point from the spring an opening is left, and the place watched ; when a herd enters, they are followed up by trained elephants with their drivers ; these get on each side of a wild one, and with strong ropes they are bound together and driven out ; they are kept tethered for some weeks, when they become tame and fitted for work.

The capturing time is most exciting. A large number of men are employed to make a terrific noise, yelling, screeching and drumming, to frighten the animals into close quarters ; sometimes they turn upon the men and give chase, but those accustomed to it seldom receive injury, they betake themselves to the shelter of a tree trunk, or a clump of bamboos, and though within a couple of yards of the pursuing elephant, they escape unobserved by keeping *perfectly still* : the slightest movement would result in their being trampled to death. The elephant, evidently aware of their close proximity, kicks up the ground in anger, and runs away. Of course, many escape from the "Poong" when there are a large number and no tame elephants enough to capture them.

Sometimes drives are conducted by torch-light, and these are likely to be successful on account of the elephant's great fear of fire. This fear sometimes puts the traveller in danger, especially in the dry season when jungle fires are burning, a *frightened* elephant is quite *mad*, and may rush into the jungle to the peril of his rider. A painful instance of this madness occurred in Assam not long ago: a Government officer was riding his own elephant, when she took fright and dashed her master to the ground, stamped on him, and thrust her tusks into him, and before she could be got off, inflicted fatal wounds. Elephants are naturally very timid, the sound of a horse's hoof or the bark of a dog is sufficient to startle them, but they are of a very uncertain temper, shewing great timidity at one time, and the reverse at another; this is troublesome to sportsmen and not every elephant can be trusted in the field. Sportsmen secure themselves from the grasp of a tiger by sitting inside a high box, called a *Houdah*, which is securely lashed above the Guddee, on the back of the elephant. Usually two or more elephants go in company to make the sport lively. Those fond of this amusement may be interested in a description of a hunt in the Goalpara district.

"The late Raja, or Zemindar of Lukhimpore, possessed a splendid elephant; he had but one tusk, but that was a beauty. Mainah had been born in captivity and remained so till he was twenty years old, when he suddenly disappeared, apparently determiued on seeing elephant life in the jungle. There was great grief in the Zemindari, for he had been born on the same day as the eldest son of his owner, and the Brahmins had foretold that as long as he remained in their possession the family would be prosperous. Every search was made and large rewards offered, but in vain; two years after, one day, he was found in his shed, as docile as when he went away. He had had an immense quantity of game shot off him, some fifty tigers, and many rhinoceri and buffaloes, and he was known to be one of the staunchest of elephants.

M. and I were anxious to kill a rhinoceros, and obtained the loan of Mainah for a hunt. We left Goahati the 29th of April, reached Barpetta May 5th; Sonapilly the 6th, where rhinoceri are generally numerous. We sallied forth, and whilst hunting for a wounded deer, we were charged by five buffaloes we had not seen. Mainah rolled over one big bull that rushed on him, and M. killed it cleverly; whilst the others, after scattering our line, turned their attention on me; though I emptied my battery of four heavy rifles, my elephant only escaped being gored by her superior speed, for she had been a famous 'Kunku' and could foot it with the best. As the country had been disturbed by a party of elephant-catchers, we moved on to Basbarree; on the way we came across a rhinoceros and killed it, also her young one unfortunately, as these are easily tamed, and worth from £60 to £100."

The country ponies are very small, and most of those owned by the Assamese, for riding or burden bearers, are cruelly treated and wretched objects. A short-legged sturdy breed of ponies are brought from Manipure, especially for the favourite game of Polo, Hocky, and sometimes for sale. Bhutan ponies are strong and serviceable; many fine imported horses are kept by Europeans for riding, driving, or racing, but they require great care to thrive in this climate.

The ryots usually keep buffaloes or oxen to plough their fields, and cows for their calves and milk; this, they only eat as curd.

Pigs are kept only by Cacharis, Mirees and hill people.

Goats are kept by all classes for the kids especially; the male kids are offered in sacrifice to the gods.

Fowls, which are the main dependence of Europeans for animal food, are chiefly raised by Mahomedans ; to the Hindu they are unclean animals, but they make a strange distinction in favourof ducks and geese ; many of these are used in sacrifice.

Assam abounds in snakes, many of a deadly kind, and a frightful number die annually from their bite. Clumps of bamboos are favourite places for them, and these abound in the jungle and in gardens. Natives are more exposed to danger than Europeans, because they go barefooted and often sleep on the ground, where they are exposed to snakes crawling into the hut at night. Floors, four or five feet high, however, are not exempt, as we know from experience, even from the most deadly kind ; the cobra may be found coiled up under furniture, or in a corner of the bathroom; another species, the Python, may be found in the fowl-house eating eggs or swallowing chickens whole.

In this country it is not quite safe to move about the house in the dark, or go out of doors without a lantern. Snake-charmers, always Hindustanee men, traverse the province in the cold season with baskets of snakes swung on their shoulders, tooting a small fife as they go along, till called on to exhibit. They lift a cloth from the top of a basket, and up springs a veritable cobra ; with a waving motion of his hand, and the shrill music of his fife, he excites the snake to spread his hood and dart his fangs at his hand ; if hit, he pretends to cure it by rubbing the spot with a snake-stone. For " buckshish " he will offer to bring a snake out of your own premises, and does it so cleverly that it seems a real fact.

There are a great variety of ground and house lizards ; a small species that creep over the house walls are quite harmless, and useful in devouring musquitoes and other insects.

Rats and mice are very numerous everywhere, and most destructive pests in every house unless hunted by cats. A large kind commit depredations in bamboo plantations. Ants, large and small, black and red, swarm everywhere, nearly every thing edible, and especially anything sweet, must be kept isolated, by being placed on a table with each leg in a cup of water, or castor oil, and this is only a safeguard when clean ; a tiny bit of dirt will be utilized as a bridge by an innumerable army in a short time.

The ravages of white ants are well known ; it is a tiny insect, like a maggot with a yellow head, armed with a powerful pair of nippers ; get one on your hand and you may pull his body off his head, but he does not let go his grip of your flesh. No house built of wood withstands long their ravages ; they turn to

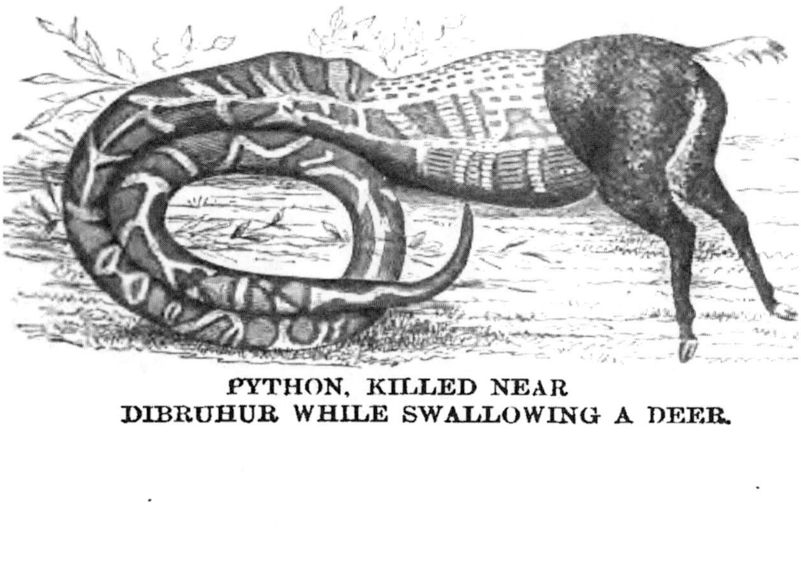

PYTHON, KILLED NEAR
DIBRUHUR WHILE SWALLOWING A DEER.

dust the largest posts, build a mud covered walk up to the roof beams, and there do the same thing. On account of these insects, houses need annual repairs to ensure their safety in a blast of strong wind, or an earthquake, both of which are likely to test it in the course of a year.

It is quite surprising what these busy little insects will do in a very short time; only a day or two is needed to riddle through a chest of clothes, turning the entire contents into shreds, and this too, while the chest is under your eye, and you can see nothing to indicate what is going on by the army of marauders who have quietly entered the bottom. In *one* night, a gentleman's trousers, left hanging over a chair, were destroyed.

At certain stages, they swarm out of their nests in the ground *winged*, and fill the air, and are very troublesome about a lamp in the evening; at such times the crows have a "*feast of fat things*," for they are a mass of fat: the hill people eat them; the *queen* is a great delicacy with the Cacharis.

Musquitoes are very troublesome for about eight months of the year, and oblige every one to sleep under a curtain. Centipedes are common, but scorpions are seldom seen except in some particular locality. Leeches are very numerous in the rains; natives, travelling with bare legs through wet places, carry a sharp-edged stick with which, every now and again, they scrape the leeches from their shins.

Fish are in great variety and abundant in every river, pond, tank, bheel, and ditch; with the Hindu it is his only animal food, and, therefore, always in great demand, but the trade is limited to *one* caste; any caste can fish for personal consumption, but on no account will any one *sell* fish but Dôms. In consequence there is often great scarcity in the market when the Dôms are busy with rice planting. Government sell the fisheries annually at auction. The best fish, those esteemed by Europeans, is the Roe, Hal, the Indian herring called Hilsa, and the Pabho. Nets are usually used for fishing in rivers, and various shaped baskets are used by groups of women in ponds and ditches.

BOTANY.

CHAPTER XV.

This most interesting feature of Assam will be treated briefly, lest our glimpse be too extended, and especially, because the writer is not qualified to do more.

The Province in every part abounds with the wildest and most luxuriant vegetation ; it is a paradise of ferns and orchids of great variety and beauty. Indigenous trees are gorgeous with flowers in every hue of the rainbow. Fruit abounds of different kinds for every month of the year.

Extensive forests furnish useful timbers in great variety; some that will bear comparison with the Teak of Burmah, or the Mahogany of other lands. The 'Ajar,' 'Sam,' 'Sissu,' 'Sol,' 'Nahor,' 'Sopa' and the 'Gohora,' resembling Teak, are all durable timbers for house or bridge building.

The 'Gomari,' 'Otenga' 'Sonali,' 'Poma' and 'Amari' are also useful timbers for a great variety of purposes, but not as durable.

In the Goalpara district, the 'Hal' is brought down in large rafts to Eastern Bengal ; this timber is valued for its durability, posts of it lasting fifty years : it is also used to make large trading boats holding one hundred and fifty tons.

Some kinds of timber trees grow to an enormous size, the trunks measuring twelve to eighteen feet in circumference, and reach a corresponding height.

The "Nahor" is an ornamental tree, growing in a cone shape, with dark green thick foliage, and large white blossoms. Date trees also beautify a garden, but the fruit here is useless.

Forest trees give the people a great variety of acid fruits which they relish as a condiment in curry : the "Bogari," "Nagatenga," "Miritenga," oranges, limes, pumeloes, citrons, and a number of small acid fruits.

Tamarind and Pappiya, are common fruits in gardens. Plantain trees are in every man's garden; they bear fruit all the year round, and are of many kinds ; the "Malbhoog" is a favourit kind ; the "Jahaje," "Sampa," "Hunda Monuhor" are also very good ; the "Jati," "Pura," "Bhim" are coarser kinds, but of ten preferred by the Assamese. The trees thrive without care, bear one bunch of fruit only, then fall, or are cut down, and new shoots spring up from the roots ; each bunch of fruit weighs from ten to forty pounds ; on each stem are from five to ten clusters, and in each cluster eight to ten plantains. At the end of the fruit stem depends a large red heart shaped flower scape, which is eaten as a vegetable. A few broad leaves droop gracefully from the top ; these are utilized by the people to furnish their guests with plates at a feast or wedding ; the middle stem is removed, and the sides, ten or twelve inches wide with a surface as smooth as glass when torn into square pieces, serve the purpose admirably. The trunk of the tree is torn into strips and dried, then burnt to make lye, used often as a substitute for salt. Mangoe trees thrive well, but the fruit is inferior to that grown in Western India, it is usually bored by insects. Custard apple, soursop, and bulls-heart, are delicious fruit. Peaches, plums and strawberries, though not indigenous, thrive well, and with good care, fine fruit is obtained. The China "letshe" thrives here, and the fruit is highly esteemed by every one ; Jack-fruit, as large as water-melons, is very sweet, and grows on the trunk, or large branches of the tree. Natives are very fond of the fruit, but it is rarely eaten by English people. The flowers of some trees, and the leaves of others, are used as a vegetable by the people.

The flowers of the "Butea frodosa" make a valuable dye, Lac insects are often found on the branches.

The bark of the Odal makes a strong rope used in capturing wild elephants. The bark of the Sonal is used for tanning.

The leaves of a plant called Jetuka, a species of

myrtle, are used to dye the inside of the hands, and the finger and toenails red, at the time of the Behufestival.

Bamboo, a large species of grass, is the most useful growth in the country, and fortunately the most abundant, it is an excellent substitute for timber in house building, and for innumerable other purposes. Bamboo forms the frame-work of nearly all native houses, split rattan being used to tie the frame together, and jungle grass for thatching; all these materials can be had simply for the labour of cutting and bringing.

The loom, the spinning wheel, the fishing tackle, the carts, yokes, and most of the conveniences of the house and field are made up of bamboo.

They grow from a creeping root from twelve to twenty feet in diameter, which sends up numerous shoots, each clump containing from twenty to one hundred bamboos; they are not firm enough for use till four or five years old; half the clump may be cut away, and new shoots spring up to supply their place, rising rapidly, perfectly straight in a few weeks, they reach a height of eighteen or twenty feet. The joints throw out a few slender stiff branches on which long grass-like leaves thicken toward the top. A full clump swaying its lofty feathery head in the breeze, is a beautiful sight.

They only flower when several years old, and these are rarely seen, as they are cut before this occurs. New shoots are eaten as a vegetable. The "Janthi" variety is thin, and easily split into strips that are used for roofing, fencing, lattice windows, sieves, &c. The "Baluka," a large strong kind, is used for posts and beams. The "Katak" is a small thorny species, quite solid, and on this account it is useful for the shafts of spears used by the Nagas. The "Bezal" is peculiar for the great length of the joints, rising from fifty to seventy feet high, straight as a needle, and from six to twelve inches in circumference, like a giant fishing rod.

There are a number of small species growing wild, the "Deum," "Tadlu," "Bejalu," "Nol," "Shagal," "Kamka" and "Parvi," some are distinguished for being straight and strong, others for being thin and easily worked into mats and baskets.

Rattan is one of the most useful products of the jungle; it grows luxuriantly in low rich soil in all parts of the province, and is used for all the purposes of a rope or string, also for platting into mats and baskets; it is excessively thorny, the stem and even the leaves are covered with horns as sharp as needles which render it a difficult matter to cut, especially for natives whose limbs are unprotected with clothing. It is a vine that winds and tangles about the trees and jungle plants to a considerable length with long brass-like glistening leaves.

There are six varieties, the "Jantre" is the most common; the slender "Pakara" is used for switches, the "Houka," strong and thick, for walking sticks; it grows to an immense length and is used for suspension bridges on mountain passes; the "Gutikhua" bears a nut eaten as substitute for betel-nut.

The palm-trees of all kinds are noted for their graceful beauty; the betel-nut is the most numerous in Assam, every one have these trees in their gardens, often in thick groves. The trunk is a slender, perfectly straight pillar, without branch or leaf, to the height of forty or fifty feet; long graceful leaves droop from the top; just under them a plume-like cluster of fine white blossoms bursts from a spath, or sheath, in which they were completely encased; then follows a bunch of two or three hundred dark green nuts about the size of a hen's egg; they turn yellow in ripening, but are usually eaten in the green state, with a little lime on the leaf of a pepper vine; often a little tobacco is added. This combination is apparently a daily necessity of every man and woman without distinction of caste; it is the wine set before a guest, or caller, the card of invitation to a wedding, and a token of constant friendship; coolies while at work must take time to take a fresh cud of "Tamul" several times in a day.

The Fan Palm "Toko," with its large circular

leaves is abundant, the leaves are not only used for fans, but to make "Japis," broad hats, to shield from rain or sun, and for boat roofs. The Sago and Cocoanut palms thrive well, but are not numerous.

The Cautchouc, or India Rubber tree, is found in great numbers in the forests, they are the largest trees in the country, many of magnificent proportions; the trunk of one measured 74 feet, the area covered by the branches 610 feet, and the height 100 feet.

A few years ago there was a successful Rubber Factory at Tezpore, carried on by a European. Rubber forests are now being planted out by Government. The hill tribes obtain a fine black varnish for their knife handles from a forest tree.

The "Hamilt" yields a wood oil used in painting. The bark of the "Sache" is used as parchment, on which their ancient histories and shasters were written.

A tree called "Bhella" bears a nut that contains an indelible ink, used for marking clothes. The bark of the "Madder" and "Asu" furnish a red dye. The red powder, the people throw on each other at the Holee festival, is made of the bark of the "Bhomrutti," it is also used as a dye.

Many wild plants are useful in the manufacture of thread or cordage.

The bark of the Rhea plant makes a strong thread, easily bleached; it is woven into warm blankets, and also used for fishing nets. The Nagas weave sheets of a species of nettle. Cotton cultivation is confined to the hills. Hemp is grown only for the flowers and leaves which are made into a drug called *bhang;* when smoked it has a more intoxicating effect than opium. Government holds the monopoly of the sale. The bark of the "Hibiscus cannabimus" is used for cordage, and the flowers and leaves as a vegetable.

The Jute of commerce, is not grown to any extent in Assam.

The trees and plants on which the silk-worms are fed, mostly grow wild. The Sum on which the Muga worm is reared is found in groves, and has three crops of leaves annually; the Mezenkure or Addakuri, is a tree from which the finest quality of silk is produced.

The Eri worm thrives best on the Castor-oil plant, the Mulberry worm is also fed on it, and for this purpose the plant is often seen in gardens.

The Lac producing insect is found on the Jura, a fig tree.

The coarse grass used for thatching roofs covers many acres of waste land in every part of the province, growing from four to six feet high. The people are at liberty to cut it anywhere either for their own use, or for sale; it is tied in bundles, brought in boat loads, and sold by the thousand. Roofs are made by spreading this thickly on a bamboo frame-work, tying it down with strips of bamboo and rattan strings; this forms a good water shed for four or five years.

Ryots usually have a patch of Tobacco plants for their own consumption, either to eat with betel-nut, or smoke. It is sold in the bazar in the form of large dry leaves for the former purpose, and chopped fine and mixed with treacle, and made into balls for smoking. The common pipe is a long tube fitted to a hole in a cocoanut shell that is partly filled with water; a small earthen cup is placed on the end of the tube containing the tobacco and live coal; the smoke is drawn through a second hole in the cocoanut shell, and in passing makes a bubbling noise in the water, this has given it the name of a hubble-bubble.

A field of sugar-cane is usually attached to every farm, and in February, when the crop is reaped, the creak of the rude sugar mill may be heard at dawn in the morning, doing the crushing of the cane for the whole village.

Medicinal plants are very numerous; there is no ailment of the human body, but the native doctor has a remedy among the trees of the forest, or the wild plants of the jungle. There is, no doubt, healing virtue in many of these remedies, but their practical application is mostly a secret of the faculty, the people generally are extremely ignorant how to treat themselves in sickness, some of the common remedies are the "Croton Tiglium" given for a cathartic, the flowers of the Mandar, and Kola Tuloki, to cure fits and convulsions ; long pepper is indigenous and used medicinally for various infirmities. The leaves of "Bagbarinda" and "Akund" are applied instead of mustard or blisters.

Native agriculture consists chiefly in rice cultivation, of which a description has been given. The Ahu crop is reaped in June and July, the Hali, November and December. There are said to be sixty varieties of rice ; that in general use is the Hali, a coarse rice usually boiled in the husk, and when cleaned is called "Ohua ;" Jahor is a finer quality. Europeans usually use Goalpara rice. Dhâl, a small pea, of which there are several varieties, is a product of every farm and enters largely into the people's diet. Mustard seed is largely cultivated, as the oil is universally used for cooking purposes, and for lamps, also to anoint their bodies. Teel, grown on the hills, is largely used in sweetmeats.

Chillies or red pepper, and ginger, are cultivated to some extent, and large quantities are brought from the hills. Turmeric, the Indian saffron, onions, garlic, and other ingredients of the universal Indian dish, curry, are raised by farmers.

The Hindu, if he has not fish, depends on various

kinds of "Haksak," pot-herbs, either wild or cultivated; as a receptacle for the oil and seasoning of *curry*, the new curled leaves of an edible fern, young leaves of Arum, and other wild plants answer the purpose.

The potatoe is supplied to the province mostly from the Khassiah hills.

The Mirees, in Upper Assam, raise large quantities of sweet potatoes. The market is usually well supplied with vegetables in their season, yams, gourds, pumpkins, cucumbers, melons, egg-plants, radishes, and a variety of native greens.

English vegetables thrive well in the dry season, and almost every European takes advantage of the fact to supply his table with these comforts.

CACHAR AND SYLHET.

CHAPTER XVI.

When the Chief Commissionership of Assam was formed in 1874, the districts of Cachar and Sylhet were added to the jurisdiction of the province ; formerly they were a part of Bengal.

Cachar is separated from the valley of the Bramaputra by the Naga hills, and Sylhet by the Khassia and Jantea hills ; both districts are watered by the Barak and Surma rivers, with their numerous tributaries flowing from the mountain ranges. These districts have a greatly diversified surface of hills, valleys and swamps.

In Sylhet eight ranges of hills run north and south, covered with dense jungle. In Cachar, the Bariel range forms a wall along the northern boundary, from 2,500 to 6,000 feet high ; from these hills numerous rivers flow into the Barak. Silchar, on the Barak, is the civil station of Cachar, and Sylhet, on the north bank of the Surma, the civil station of Sylhet.

Cachar has an area of 3,750 square miles, and a population of 313,858, Sylhet has an area of 5,383 square miles, and a population of 1,969,000.

Tea was discovered indigenous in Cachar in 1855, and the first garden started the same year ; the following year it was discovered in Sylhet, and at present both districts are largely occupied by Tea planters. Tea gardens are cultivated mostly on the low hills, and on the undulating surface south of the Barak, also on plateau land.

The progress of this industry in Cachar will be indicated by the following statistics : in 1869 the area under cultivation was reported at 24,151 acres, with an outturn of 4,234,794 lbs. ; in 1874, area under cultivation 30,066 acres, outturn of Tea, 5,974,829 lbs.

Sylhet produces much less than Cachar : in 1868 the area under cultivation in that district was 2,050 acres, and the outturn at 250,906 lbs. ; in 1874 the area was 19,190 acres, and outturn 565,567 lbs. In the Sruma valley there was an outturn in 1882 of 17,383,136 lbs.

The great depression, which followed excessive speculation in 1865, affected these districts equally with the Brahmaputra valley, but since that time progress has been steady, and at the present time Cachar leads the list of Tea-producing districts, the outturn in 1883 having been 12,721,327 lbs.

The chief industry of the natives in Cachar, is cotton spinning and weaving. The raw cotton is first dried in the sun, then to remove the seeds, it is passed through a rude instrument, consisting of two small wooden cylinders, placed parallel to each other and close together ; with a handle on one side these are put in motion with the right hand, while with the left, the cotton is passed between them, the seeds falling on the inner side ; the cotton is then made soft and light by striking it with a bow string ; it is then made into balls, by rolling it on a stick and then withdrawing the stick. The ball, now ready for spinning, is fixed on the point of an iron rod, which is used as a spindle ; with the left hand a thread is drawn out, and by twirling the rod, it winds around it ; when there is sufficient on the rod, it is taken off, and this yarn is ready for weaving.

The loom is a primitive instrument, the warp is placed lengthwise, and the woof, on a wooden shuttle, is shot in with the hand.

In the Sylhet district, the Manipuri women weave very fine coverlets and handkerchiefs, embroidering the edge with silk very tastefully.

The pottery of Sylhet is noted for its beauty in form and design ; a great deal of attention is paid also to the production of Lac ; it is manufactured into bracelets and many beautiful articles of ornamentation. A speciality of the district is the manufacture of a fine smooth matting from the bark of a wild plant; the mats are very durable and made of all sizes, and to be found in the bazars every where in Assam. Another speciality is ivory carving, in which the people show great taste and skill; their ivory mats are sold as high as from £20 to £60 each. They cut solid shell bracelets from the conch shell, which are much prized and very fine.

The wild animals of these districts are the same as are found in the Bramaputra valley. Tigers, leopards and different species of deer abound. The hill tracts watered by the Singlai and Langai, are the rendezvous of wild elephants, and every year many are captured; the formation of a Keddah or trap, enclosing about five acres, involves considerable expense, and about a month is required to construct a strong palisade, inside of which a ditch is dug three cubits wide, and two deep; two or three hundred men are employed to surround their place of rendezvous, who by drumming and shouting, frighten the herd into the Keddah, they are followed by trained elephants, each with a rider, who wedge a wild one between them, then the rider goes underneath and fastens the wild elephant's feet to a tree. This done they secure another; sometimes the animals become frantic at finding themselves secured, and injure themselves or others so much that they die.

Tigers are numerous in the Sylhet district, not

withstanding Government give a liberal reward for each one captured. Capturing them alive is made a a source of amusement, a description of which we quote from the appendix in Dr. Hunter's statistics, contributed by a resident in the district. "We caught from fifty to sixty tigers annually which afforded us much amusement; large traps, constructed of wood and turf, not less than thirty feet long, with four doors successively opening from each other, are built in such places as the tigers frequent ; the bait is a living bullock in the centre ; the tiger may enter at either end ; on treading on a spring the two counter doors drop, and *he* is secured while the bullock remains in perfect safety. A tube or cylinder, about twelve feet long and eighteen inches calibre, made of mats and fortified with ropes or rattan, and secured at the further end by sticks across it, is introduced into the trap, and the tiger being previously teased and very anxious to escape, seeing this ray of daylight conveyed into his prison through the tube, gathers himself together and darts into in the hope of finding a passage at the opposite extremity, but is stopped by the crossbars ; a man stands by to drive in two other bars across the end by which he entered. No mouse was ever more inoffensive than this powerful animal now finds himself; the whole space he has to move in is only eighteen inches calibre, which barely allows him to move, and I have frequently taken him by the whiskers with impunity. But his troubles are not at an end. He is now lifted on a cart and conveyed to the town; the place chosen for his public *debut*, was generally an old mosque surrounded by a high wall, enclosing half an acre of ground. In this enclosure a buffalo awaits his arrival, and stages are erected for spectators to see the sport. It matters little whether the buffalo is wild or tame, in either case, he has the same antipathy to the tiger, and attacks him whenever they meet; in the present instance, the buffalo was a tame one, brought from his usual occupation in the field and submissive to his driver, but the moment the tiger entered, his character changed; he foamed at the mouth with rage, and with fury attacked his opponent; the tiger put himself on the defensive, threw himself on his back, biting and tearing the limbs of his antagonist, but the buffalo soon over powered him and threw him in the air, tossing him from horn to horn with wonderful dexterity until he was dead.

The leopard shows much more play when he is put into the pen with a buffalo; in an instant he is on the top of his back and makes him completely furious; he jumps from limb to limb, wounding him in every direction, but whenever the buffalo can hit him a fair blow he is done for.

The Lushais, a hill poople, south of Cachar, have given in past years a deal of trouble by frequent raids on peaceful villages in British territory, making it necessary for the Government to send several expeditions to punish their lawlessness and make stipulations with them to keep the peace, which of late years they seem to have regarded. The Oacharee race was originally a hill people, occupying the hills north of the Brahmaputra, and comprised a large and powerful kingdom; they claim a list of one hundred and three independent sovereigns, commencing with Ghatikuch Nariyan, son of Bhim, a hero of the Mahabharata, but this ancient history is styled "a Brahminical forgery."

"The history is traced as far back as 1700, when they settled at Kashpur on the southern spurs of the Bariel range. On certain great occasions, it was the custum to offer *human* sacrifices to the king."

The present military cantonments in Silchar contain an area of 140 acres; it is the head-quarters of a native infantry, and several European officers. The climate of these districts does not materially differ from that of the Brahmaputra valley, a dry and rainy season, or what corresponds to it, a cold and hot season; the latter commencing in April and lasting till October; the heaviest rainfall occurring in June, July and August. With the entering of the cold season come dense fogs every morning, lasting to ten or eleven o'clock, when the eaves and trees drip as if in a gentle sprinkle of rain.

Education in Cachar is of recent date, in 1857 there was not a school in the district, now they number one hundred and thirty-five with 4,434 pupils.

Sylhet was in a similar condition till the reform inaugurated by Sir George Campbell in 1872, in extending the grant-in-aid rules to village schools; the report for 1883 gives to the district four hundred and four schools, with 15,561 pupils.

HILL TRIBES.

CHAPTER XVII.

THE Brahmaputra valley is enclosed in a deep range of hills. North of the Durrung and Kamrup districts are the Bhutea, Akas and Duphla ranges; south, the Khassia and Jantia ranges; north of Lukimpore, the Miree and Mishmi ranges; southerly the Naga hill range, extending south of the Sibsagar and Nowgong districts; and south of the Goalpara district, are the Garo hills.

The names of the hill ranges by no means represent the languages spoken by the people. The Naga hill people are divided into many clans, each speaking a distinct language, and to these must be added the Khamptis, Singphos, Lalongs, Mirees, Abors, Migis and others.

Each of these tribes is quite distinct in physique and habits, as well as language, and that this is the case in so small an area, is quite remarkable, and a subject for philological research.

We will take a glimpse of the people, beginning at the southern point.

The population of the Garo hills is estimated at from eighty to one hundred thousand.

Only a part of the hill country was subject to British rule up to 1872. On account of frequent raids on British subjects, an expedition was sent into the hills, which resulted in bringing the entire Garo country under British control.

Though considered a rude, illiterate people, their language is capable of some nice distinctions as illustrated by the following: "A missionary was in doubt about the different shades of meaning in the two words *ching* and *aching* used for the pronoun, we, till one day he used *aching* in a confession of sin in public prayer; he was told afterwards that he used the wrong word as *aching* included the person addressed; it was discovered that *aching* is a contraction of *naching*, which is rarely used, a compound of *nao*, you, and *ching*, we, which explains the peculiarity in the use.

They are a robust, active race, cultivating chiefly rice and cotton; men and women carry their produce to the plains in long baskets on their backs, held by a strap across the forehead, the burden weighing from eighty to one hundred pounds. Their weapons are a spear and sword, the latter, a kind peculiar to the tribe. It is two-edged, the blade and handle form one piece; it also serves the purpose of agriculture; in warfare, they carry shields, with a supply of bamboo spikes inside. They are not hunters, but snare birds and beasts; they trap an elephant by attaching a string to a loaded spear placed in a tree.

They are inveterate smokers, and indulge freely in rice beer, which is not strong, but when taken in large quantities, it intoxicates.

Though the tribe is divided into many clans, they are not independent of each other; the chiefs of the different clans assemble in council, and decide the political affairs of the people.

They build their houses on piles; are not in the least fastidious about their food; cats, dogs, frogs and snakes are all acceptable, but for one of the *best* things—milk, they have a great abhorrence.

The ordinary clothing of both men and women is a narrow bit of cloth around the loins; the women are considered very ugly in appearance; they wear a profusion of rude ornaments,—twenty or thirty strings of beads and bell-metal ornaments about their necks; in their ears brass rings of a pound weight; frequently, the ear lobe is torn through by the weight; this they think something to be proud of, and the rings are not dispensed with, but hung by a string over the head. Men and women sometime wear a sheet over the shoulders; the poor make the sheet of the bark of a tree, by soaking it and then beating it out soft.

They never cut their hair, but wind it up in knots

with a piece of cloth. The men have no beards, but wear around their heads a string of brass plates.

Parents contract the marriages of their children, but the ceremony is not performed till they are of marriageable age. The bridegroom is taken to the house of the bride by his friends ; a cock and hen are offered in sacrifice, and the entrails consulted for an omen ; whether good or bad, the marriage takes place.

The priest strikes the woman on the back with the dead cock, and the man with the hen, when they are pronounced man and wife. Feasting and dancing follow : "Their mode of dancing is peculiar. Twenty or more men, behind one another in a row, hold each other by their belts, then go round in a circle, hopping first no one foot, then on the other, singing and keeping time with the music, which is animating though inharmonious ; the women also dance in rows, holding out their hands, lowering one, and raising the other, as the music beats, occasionally turning round with great rapidity."

The married man literally " forsakes father and mother and cleaves unto his wife ;" he lives in *her* family and becomes one of *her* clan. A singular custom prevails, by which a man who marries a favourite daughter, in the event of the death of his father-in-law, must marry his mother-in-law, and through *her* succeeds to all the property, which only descends through the female line. Sons must look to the family into which they marry for their establishment in life.

The *wife* is the head of the family. Garo women enjoy a power and position equal to anything that could be desired by the advocates of woman's rights.

Their religious ideas are similar to other hill people. They are not idolaters, but profess to believe in a Supreme Being they call "*Saljong*," who is impersonated in the sun, but they do not worship it: their troubles are attributed to some evil spirit whom they try to propitiate by sacrifices. The idea is prevalent, that some persons have the power of leaving the human frame, and taking up their abode in a tiger or other animal.

The body of the dead is laid out in its best clothes, and kept for three days, then burned on a pile built a few yards from the house; the ashes are collected in a vessel which is placed on top of the pile; this is enclosed by a fence, and food and drink are placed on it for the journey of the departed to "Chikmong," a hill north of Sosong, where they believe the departed spirit has a resting place.

The Khassias occupy a range of hills extending from the Garo hills to Manipure on the east, bordering Sylhet on the north, and forming part of the Cachar district. One of the hills, Shillong is the residence of the chief officers of Government and the sanitarium of the province.

The people are cheerful in disposition, laborious, and in moral character, above their neighbours; though usually peaceable, when they suppose their rights invaded, they rise in rebellion, as was the case in 1830 and in 1862.

Though very illiterate, they are apt to learn, and schools among them are well sustained.

They show great ingenuity in constructing a bridge across a mountain stream: they bring the roots and branches of a fig tree together, and by interweaving them, a strong living bridge is formed.

Their religious ideas are very similar to the Garos; their marriages are not arranged by the parents, but by the parties themselves, and on the day fixed for their union, they are simply asked if they will take each other, and a reply being given in the affirmative, they are declared married.

They enclose their dead in a box before cremation; a procession and a funeral dirge, played on bamboo flutes, follows the remains, and gives solemnity to the occasion. The Cacharees are a peaceable, hardy and industrious race, of migratory habits. Besides the Cachar district and the Chatgari division of the Durrung district, they are found all over the province in small settlements ; many are employed on the Tea gardens ; they are much stronger than emigrants from Bengal, but are extremely clanish, and frequently give the planters trouble.

In the hills their own language is spoken, and though those living on the plains understand Assamese, among themselves they use their own tongue. Their language is said to have no word to express a number above eight, indicating the extreme ignorance of the people.

They seldom cultivate the same piece of land more than three years ; they regularly irrigate their fields and raise large crops of rice, mustard seed, &c.: their forests yield a large quantity of sticklac.

On the hills bordering on Bhutan, they are called Mechs. In their habits, they are uncleanly, and not at all particular what they eat; pork they are especially fond of, and one never sees a few Cacharree huts without pigs.

Their religion consists in a belief in a god, and in many evil spirits who must be appeased with sacrifices; many in the plains have become so far Hinduised, that they will not eat beef or drink liquor. That they have a willing ear for instruction is evident from the numbers that have joined the S. P. G. Mission, and also become connected with the Baptist

Missions. Their marriage ceremony preserves "the primitive form of forcible abduction." The bridegroom goes to the house of his intended with a company of friends; her friends endeavour to retain her; a mock combat ensues in which, of course, the bridegroom is victorious. He gives a sum of money to conciliate the bride's father who is *supposed* to be opposed; the usual feasting and dancing follow, and the affair is complete.

The women perform a large share of the labor necessary to support the family; they work in the fields, carry wood and water, cook and take care of children, and weave most of the clothing.

The virgin soil yields abundantly, waste land is plentiful, and everything necessary to their simple wants is easily obtained. Their houses are raised on piles, built with a timber frame, a bamboo floor, and the whole tied together with rattan, or stalks of cardamom; the whole house frequently encloses but one room, that serves all the purposes of the family; the pigs, fowls, &c., herd under the floor. The Mikeers and Lalongs occupy the hills southerly and westerly, in the Nowgong district, and outnumber the Assamese. They are estimated to number 34,000. The Lalongs resemble the Cacharees in customs and religion; many have adopted Hinduism.

Mikeers mostly keep to their simple faith in one

supreme being whom they call "Hempatin," they sacrifice fowls or pigs to evil spirits; many have become believers in Christ, and professed their faith in baptism and been formed into churches.

A number of young men are being educated at the Normal School in Nowgong, of the American Baptist Mission. Their marriage customs are similar to the adjacent hill tribes; a young man chooses for himself and sends some friends with a pot of rice-liquor to make the proposal; if the party agree, the day is fixed for the nuptials, which always takes place at the bride's house, accompanied by the usual feasting, with a liberal supply of rice-liquor. The groom remains in the house of the bride for a year or two, then builds a house for himself.

Polygamy is not permitted among them. The mode of rice-liquor manufacture is presumably similar to that of other hill people, who all indulge in the use of it. The rice is soaked in water for some days, then the water is pressed out, and the rice made into little cakes that are hung in the smoke for a week; when they are again soaked in the water for a day or two, then the liquor is ready for use.

They are an industrious people, raising large quantities of cotton, rice and Erea thread.

The women share largely in all the labors of the field, in addition to their household duties; they are very strong, and bear heavy burdens on their backs. From the villages on the outskirts of Goahati, these Mikeer women may be seen every day bringing heavy loads of wood to sell, on their backs held by a strap across the forehead; often with the addition of a baby slung in a cloth on the breast. For their load they receive only three or four annas: eight or ten cents.

THE NAGAS.

CHAPTER XVIII.

THE Naga hills extend from North Cachar to the eastern undefined boundary between Assam and the Singpho country.

The name, Naga, is by some supposed to be derived from the Bengalee term "nangta," meaning naked, applicable to the people on account of the extreme scantiness of their clothing; others identify the name with the Sanskrit word, "naga," a snake.

Under the generic name of Naga are included a large number of clans who are independent of each other, and virtually independent of foreign rule. The clans are divided, under the names Namsangias, Burdwareas, Pamdwareas, Tablungeas, Mooloongeas, Changnoias, Laptangs, Kameas, Topigamias, and others. Each clan has a chief, whose authority they submit to; the office is not hereditary: when a death occurs another is chosen by the people. The different tribes resemble one another in habits and customs, though their dialects differ so much, that villages on adjacent hills can only communicate with one another in Assamese.

They all use the same weapons, a spear and "dah;

OUR BROTHER AND SISTER. NAGAS.

—a short sword used also for agricultural purposes; in warfare they carry a shield, with a supply of "pangees,"—bamboo spikes, and sometimes a crossbow and arrows. The Angamas have of late obtained firearms.

The Angamas, Rengmas and Kachas are partly in British territory; the first tribe is the most numerous and powerful, inhabiting the hills in the south-east, between the Diphupani and Maon; they are a fine looking, athletic race; with flat noses, and high cheek bones, of the Indo-Chinese stock, as are all the Naga tribe. They are brave, but vindictive and treacherous; the only *article* they wear is a dark cloth kilt,—a mere fig leaf, weighted with cowrie shells or brass ornaments; at times a sheet is thrown over the shoulders; they seem to imagine a deficiency of clothing is compensated by a profusion of ornaments on every part of the body; these are of a rude, fantastic kind, which are quite indescribable; numerous strings of beads, boars' tusks and shells are hung around the neck; the ears have several large holes in the lobe for the reception of brass rings, heavy square glass drops, ornaments made of cane and goats' hair, dyed red and yellow; when they have nothing better, they stuff a bunch of cotton in the holes; above the elbow and the wrists are armlets of cane or cowrie shells; around the waist and below the knee are many rings of black or red cane. The warrior wears a badge of honor on his breast, platted of bamboo, cane, and colored goats' hair, mingled with human hair, from the heads he has cut off. They make themselves hideous with tatooing, which is also a mark of honor for having beheaded an enemy.

Some of the clans cut their hair square in front, and tie the long hair in a knot on the back of the head, others cut it all round, leaving it long in front. A chief distinguishes himself by wearing a high cap of cane-work, decked with boars' tusks and toucan feathers, standing erect, and with a scarlet blanket over his shoulders.

The women wear a short tight skirt of dark blue cloth of their own weaving, and are less profuse than the men in ornamentation.

The clans are in constant hostility to one another: village is pitted against village, and sometimes a village contains hostile parties within itself.

"A life for a life" is the maxim put in practice among them, and every man is at liberty to take revenge; men lie in wait on the hill paths to spring upon any travellers, cut off their heads and hands, and bear them off to their village to drink, dance, and carouse around. They often do this without provocation, simply to gratify a bloodthirsty disposition, and gain *honor* among their people.

They make frequent incursions for the purpose of taking slaves, to be afterwards ransomed by their friends with cloth, cows or pigs.

At the entrance of their villages is a large building, the "Morung," where a wooden drum is kept to beat, to call the warriors together, also where their trophies of victory are hung, a "Golgotha," place of skulls; in *one, over* 350 *skulls* of men, women and children were displayed.

The Nagas have frequently come into collision with the British Government; up to 1857 no less than *ten* expeditions had been sent to repress these lawless savages, though Government officers travelled among them, and received pledges of future peaceable conduct.

A survey party was attacked in 1875, and Lieut. Holcomb, with eighty of the party were killed, and many others wounded.

In 1878 another survey party fell into an ambuscade, and Capt. Butler died from a spear wound.

The last expedition against the Angama Nagas in 1880, aroused by the murder of the civil officer, Mr. Damant, was the largest hitherto sent, and intended to settle, once for all, the submission of these savages to British control, and open their eyes to the fact that it was a power they could not cope with. They imagine their position is impregnable, and there are certainly great difficulties. The Angama villages are on the summit of the most inaccessible hills, and fortified with stockades, deep ditches and massive stone walls, the hill sides are bristling with bamboo spikes; in some cases, the sloping side of the hill is cut away so as to form a perpendicular wall. The approaches to the villages are tortuous and narrow, only wide enough to admit the passsage of *one* man at a time ; these lead to gates closed by strong heavy wooden doors, with look-outs on which a sentry is posted day and night. Often these approaches are steeply scarped, and the only means of entry is by a ladder consisting of a single pole fifteen or twenty feet high cut into steps. The last expedition besides being a very heavy expense to Government, cost the lives of some officers and a number of men, but it was so far successful, that a new Government station has been established at Kohima, a hill of one of the former hostile villages, and since the close of the campaign, peace has been maintained.

The Angamis appear to be far better provided with the necessaries of life than the tribes on the hills near Sibsagar; *they* are miserably poor, eat anything, even the carcasses of dead animals, and work very hard to obtain a bare subsistence from their hill side fields, which are often invaded by a swarm of rats that devour their crops, and subject them to actual want. They are opium-eaters, which the Angamas are not, and this is sufficient reason for their miserable condition.

The tribe generally are unclean, never bathe or wash their blankets; water is not easily obtained.* They are as uncleanly about their food; one of their greatest dainties is a dog stuffed with as much rice as possible, then roasted *alive.*

Their houses are very large, built on the ground, except where the place is uneven, a flooring is laid from rock to rock or on posts, the ridge pole nearly touching the ground and the thatched roof on each side; it is divided into two rooms, the outer one serving for all purposes during the day, the inner room is the sleeping apartment and granary; the sides are lined with wicker baskets in which grain is stored.

In the cool season, small parties come to the plains with long baskets on their backs, supported by a strap across the forehead, containing dried chillies, ginger, cotton and black salt, which they barter for salt, rice and opium.

They usually call at the bungalows and beg for liquor, which they too often get, and willingly return the favor with the exhibition of a war dance; this consists in frantic jumps and leaps, throwing their spears with wild ferocity, while they yelp, and hoot like a pack of demons.

Their fondness for liquor is a serious obstacle to the improvement of their condition; some tribes manufacture liquor from Job's tears (seed of a wild grass), others from rice or buckwheat.

The religion of the Nagas is chiefly one of fear; "the good spirits," they say, "will do us only good, but the evil spirits will trouble us unless we conciliate their favor with sacrifices." They have vague and strange ideas about a future state, some say, "if we are good we will fly above, and live in the stars; if bad, we will pass through several existences, and finally become bees;" others say, "we rot in the ground and that is the end, what do we know more?" What a revelation of the depth of ignorance and darkness, that hides a possible glorious future! Like all ignorant people, they are excessively superstitious; an omen must be sought on every occasion of importance. To ascertain whether a projected raid will be successful, a soft reed is cut into slices, if they fall one upon another, victory is certain, if scattered, the project is abandoned. In making a promise or taking an oath, the muzzle of a gun, or a spear head, is taken between the teeth and a declaration made, "If I do not perform my promise," or, "if what I say is not true, may I fall by this weapon." The most sacred oath is made by two parties taking a fowl between them, one by the head, the other by the legs, and

NAGA TRAVELLING.

pulling it asunder; intimating that by a breach of contract they would merit the same fate.

They secure game by traps and pitfalls; the pit is filled with spikes, so that the animal is transfixed killed.

On the low hills they cultivate the same land only two or three years, but the high hills are cut into terraces, irrigated and cultivated for successive years.

Their marriage customs resemble those of the other hill tribes; the following description of their customs in sickness and death will be read with interest: "The wealthiest man in the village was taken ill, his riches were in rice lands, 'Pan' gardens, pigs, cows, war habiliments, ornaments, and a quantity of cooking utensils. Although an occasional attendant at religious services, he made no pretensions to Christianity. Early in his illness he sent to Mr. C. for medicine; the disease not yielding readily, fears arose, and secretly the blood of a pig was spilled for 'Lezeba,' an evil spirit; subsequently a cow was sacrificed, but Lezeba was not propitiated; the disease raged, and more blood flowed, till a cow, five pigs, and a dog had been offered."

A soothsayer was consulted, and he informed them that a wild buffalo, another pig, and a cow, were demanded, but death was near, and the poor man again begged for medicine, but it was too late.

As is customary with the tribe, when a person dies, a dog was killed that it might accompany the spirit of the man to the future world.

The body finds its last resting place in a miniature bamboo house, on a plaform four feet high, erected on ground set apart in the jungles for the repository of the dead.

As is not unfrequently the case, this man requested that his body be dried before taking it away.

This process over a slow fire, will be continued for several weeks in his home, the family meantime occupying the house as usual.

The evening of his death, a hog was killed, and over this initiatory feast, the wife continued all night in singing the praises of her husband. On the following day two more hogs were slain for the friends who gathered to commemorate the virtues of the departed, and the villagers generally "abstained from labor in honor of the dead."

The Rengma Nagas occupy the hills between the Jamuna and Kahani rivers ; they can scarcely be distinguished from the Mikeers with whom they have intermarried.

The Kacha Nagas inhabit the southern portion of the Bariel range, between the Dhunsiri and Barak rivers ; they resemble the Angama clans, but speak a different dialect, and are less warlike and muscular.

HILL TRIBES.

CHAPTER XIX.

THE Kamptis belong to the Shan or Thai race, and are called in Burmah "Shangyai," or eldest branch of the Shans ; they have been an element of power in the history of Assam. The ruler of their country, the kingdom of Pong, bordering on Siam and Yunam, after conquering the adjoining province of Manipure, crossed the hills and eventually brought into subjection the Assam valley as far as Kamrup. Their first settlement was on the bank of the Tengapani river, afterward they pushed on to Sadiya, opposed British possession, treacherously attacked and destroyed the military station in 1839, killing Major White, and a large number of sepoys They were afterwards driven out with great slaughter. The tribe are Budhists, with temples and priests in all their villages in the south-eastern portion of the Lukimpore district. The chiefs and priests amuse themselves in carving wood, ivory and metals, and are said to excel in the art.

The Kampti dress is similar to the Burmese ; the men wear a tight fitting jacket and a nether garment of cotton or silk plaided in bright colors, flowing to the knees, a turban of white muslin twisted round the head with the long hair, forms a topknot projecting forward on the top of the head. The women bind their hair in a roll on the forehead ; their skirts are plaided in bright colors, or embroidered. They weave the family garments, and dye the thread. The women are short, stout, and very good-natured ; they use a different rice from the Assamese ; it is a glutinous kind, when cooked it is served up in round balls on a leaf.

The villagers of "Fakeyals" on the bank of the Dehing, are also Thai emigrants from the valley of the Hukong ; they strictly adhere to all the customs of their own country, and the religion of Budhism.

The Singphoos in Burmah are called Kakyens ; the name given them here, in their language, signifies *man ;* their country lies between the undefined boundary on the east of Burmah. They are an athletic, semi-civilized and industrious race; their customs resembling the Kamptees. Their features are of Mongolian type,—oblique eyes, large mouth, high cheek-bones, complexion a tawny yellow ;—married women wear their hair in a knot on the crown, fastened with silver pins and chains. The maidens gather their hair in a roll on the back of the neck and ornament it. The men tattoo their limbs, and all married women tattoo their legs from the knee to the ankle in broad bands.

Their villages contain from fifty to sixty large houses, from eighty to one hundred feet long and twenty broad, with raised floor and open verandah, where the women sit and weave or embroider.

Their language has an affinity to the Karens of Burmah, and like them, their religion consists in propitiating evil spirits, and in a belief in a Supreme Being.

They have a singular tradition, that their ancestors were once in a Paradise, where they were immortal, and held converse with celestial beings; but for some act of disobedience, they were driven out, and became debased. Who can doubt that the history of our first parents is preserved in this tradition?

For generations this tribe made raids into the valley of Assam, capturing hundreds of the people as slaves; a good number of their descendants are still found in Upper Burmah.

After British occupation, they attempted to take Sadiya, but were repulsed by Capt. Neuville, who recovered from them upwards of 5,000 Assamese slaves. They have been peaceable of late years, and are sufficiently friendly to be proposed as a medium in opening the trade route into China. The Mishmees are our most distant hill tribe neighbours, their villages extending from the Nemlong, an affluent of the Irrawadi, around the Daphabham mountain, up the valley of the Bra, to the borders of Thibet.

Small parties often come to Dibrughur for trade; they seem an inoffensive people, but are styled very keen traders.

Their country has been visited by Capt. Wilcox, Dr. Griffith and Col. Rowlitt. In 1854, two Roman Catholic priests were murdered at one of their villages, their property plundered, and a Singpho servant taken as a slave.

This conduct was avenged by an expedition dispatched by the Marquis of Dalhousie led by Lieut. Eden, who captured the Chief and his followers by surprise, recovered the plunder, and released the servant.

The mountainous country they inhabit is described as very grand and beautiful, but most difficult to travel; a path winds round steep precipices with only a narrow ledge for a foothold, and, in some places, not even this: only holes in the face of the precipice for the hands or feet. The traveller needs steady nerves to cross such a bridge, as is described by Mr. K., suspended across a roaring torrent hundreds of feet beneath.

"The point selected for these aerial bridges is where the river is most narrowly confined by rocks;

a rope made of three or four rattan strands is flung across, the extremity fastened to rocks or trees, and tightened as much as possible; on this rope, a moveable ring is fastened, of the same material. The person who has to cross, places his body in the ring, and, if necessary, his head in a small loop formed for the purpose, then with his face turned upward, he allows the ring to move; it slides rapidly to the middle, and the remaining portion of the distance the passenger accomplishes by working his way up with hands and feet."

Mishmee houses are few in a village, but of great length, that of a Chief, one hundred and thirty feet, divided into many apartments for his numerous wives and children; in one house there are often one hundred persons. They are great polygamists, every man having as many wives as he can afford to buy, the price varying from a pig to twenty oxen. On the death of a Chief all his wives become the property of his heir, except the mother of the heir who would belong to the next of kin among the males.

They are a pastoral people, and have large herds of the "Mithun," a large hill ox. They bring the poisonous root, "Aconitum ferox," to the plains for trade, and another valuable medicinal plant, "Coptis teeta," also the musk bags of the musk-deer.

Their religious customs are very like other hill

tribes; they imagine a demon the author of their sorrows whom they must reconcile with offerings, but have no idea of a good and beneficent Supreme Being. Their priests officiate at marriage and funeral ceremonies. Around the grave of the deceased they hang his clothes, his implements, and the skulls of the animals he has killed. Their costume is a narrow strip about the loins, a jacket of striped cloth reaching to the knees, made with a slit in the middle for the passage of the head, and at the sides for the arms; leather shoulder straps, with four pouches attached, a knapsack, ingeniously contrived for the back, covered with long black fibres of the Sago-palm, and decorated with the tail of the Thibetan cow, a sword-knife, dagger, spear and a fur cap completes the full costume.

The women wear a colored cloth held loosely round the waist and a very scanty bodice; on their neck a profusion of glass, cornelian and agate beads; on their heads they wear a thin silver plate, broad over the forehead, and tapering towards the ears, tied round by a chain of small shells.

Men and women wear the hair long, gathered in a knot on the brow; both sexes are great smokers; they begin at an early age and smoke all the time when not eating or sleeping. They are fair for Asiatics, short, and sturdy.

The tribe are divided into clans, the *Tain* living in the plains, the "Maro" south of the Brahmaputra, the "Misha" south-east perhaps, connected with the "Manitze," the aborigines of Younam. The "Chilikata Michmus" or Midhis are distinguished by the custom of cropping the hair across the forehead, the fashionable "bang" of ladies of civilized lands.

They have often committed raids on the villages of the plains, but their impassible country has saved them from retribution.

The tribe are particularly skilfull in weaving cloth from fibrous plants that grow in the hills; from the "Rhea nevea," andothers of the nettle species, they weave a strong stiff cloth, made into jackets, which are *worn as an armour*. This tribe use poisoned arrows, and "panjees" to obstruct the path of their enemies.

They are said to be nearly devoid of religious feeling or any ideas of God or a future state. Darkness so profound, is rarely met with, even in the wildest specimens of the human race. The Abors, Daphlas, and Akas, inhabit a range of hills on the northern side of the Brahmaputra between the valley of Assam and Thibet. The tribe north of Dibrughur call themselves "Padans."

"Membu," a large settlement on these hills, is the place where the "gams" or elders assemble at the

Morang, or town-hall, in legislative council, and discuss important matters connected with the people; the assembly generally numbers two or three hundred, besides any number of boys, who take a position of observation, and at the close, shout the decisions through the village.

The *desks* of these legislators have numerous fire-places around which they sit and smoke, drink, and make speeches.

Their religious ideas are somewhat in advance of other hill people ; they acknowledge and worship God as the Father of all, and they believe in a future state where happiness or misery will depend on their conduct in this world. They regard omens, and a bird's entrails, or a pig's liver are made to foretell future events. When an animal is sacrificed, only the poor are allowed to share the meat with the gods.

Their traditions in regard to the origin of the race, is singular and interesting. They say the human family are all descended from one common mother; she had two sons, the elder a bold hunter, the younger a cunning craftsman ; the latter was the mother's favourite. With him she migrated to the west, taking with her all the household utensils, arms, implements of all sorts, so that the art of making them was lost in the land she deserted ; but before quitting the old country, she taught her first-born how to forge *dáhs,* large knives, and to make musical instruments, and she left him a great store of blue and white beads; these beads and the simple arts known to him, he transmitted to his posterity, the Padans, and from him, they received the injunction, to mark themselves on the forehead with a *cross*. The western nations, including the English, are descended from the younger brother, and they inherited from him, and the mother, the knowledge of science and art. The Padans have no knowledge of art, except what is accounted for in the tradition.

They cultivate rice, cotton, maize, tobbaco, ginger, red pepper, sugar-cane, esculent roots and opium. Their cultivation commences from the Sheku river, the necessity of crossing which has obliged them to construct a suspension bridge. Of these, the canes form the main support, and are thrown across beams supported partly on triangles of strong timber, and partly on growing trees; these trees have stays to counteract their flexibility, and they, as also all the suspending canes, are made fast to the stumps of other large trees, or to piers of loose stone. The roadway is made of cane interlaced, supported by elliptical girders of the same material, passing around the main suspenders. The bridge is carefully repaired every year.

The Abors are a tall, strong race, with Mongolian features and copper-colored complexion. Polygamy is not practiced. Women are treated with great consideration, marriages being settled by the young people themselves. In a society where all are on an equality, and the industry of the man and wife provide them with comforts equal to their neighbours, there is no occasion for parents to manœuvre a match; to sell a child's happiness for *money*, would be considered by them a great disgrace.

The whole village unite to build a house for a new married couple; all the material is first brought and prepared, then there is a general *house-raising*—well known to new settlers in America—the men of the village all turn out to work, and in these hills a house is built and ready for occupation in *one day*

The Abor in full dress is a grotesque figure; on the loins he wears the bark of the Ujdal tree, hanging down behind in loose strips, fifteen inches long, like a white bushy tail; it is his carpet to sit on by day, or pillow at night; some wear long Thibetan cloaks; they weave a cotton cloth, with a long fleecy nap which they make into jackets. On State occasions they wear a helmet made of cane, adorned with pieces of bear's skins, yâk tails dyed red, boar's tusks, and, above all, the huge beak of the Bucerus. The hair of both males and females is cropped short; this is done by lifting it on a knife and chopping it on a stick all round.

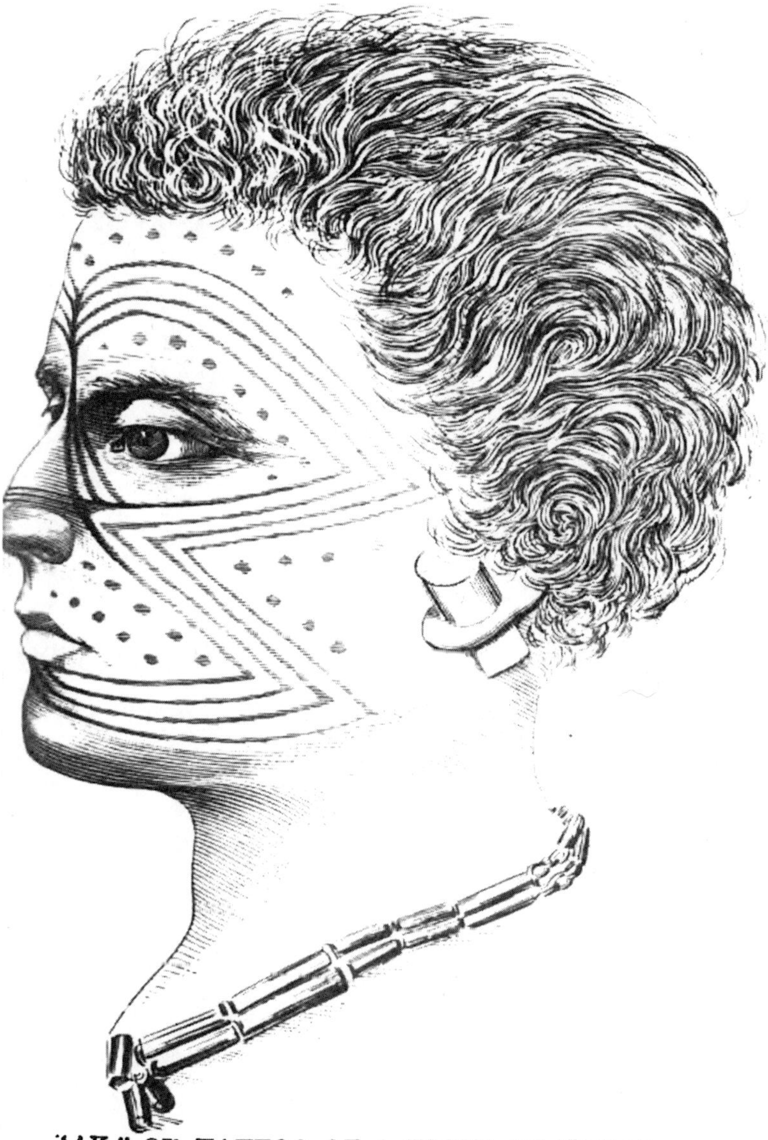

"AK," OR TATTOO OF A TRIBE OF NAGAS.

Tattooing is universal; the men wear a cross on the forehead, the women on the upper lip and on both sides of it, and stripes below the mouth. Their dress is a striped red and blue cloth petticoat held on by a girdle of cane work; sometimes another cloth is folded over the bosom. The neck is profusely ornamented with strings of bead reaching to the waist, and the lobes of the ears are filled with rude ornaments; round the ankles, to set off the fine swell of their bare legs, broad bands of very finely plaited cane work are tightly laced.

All females with pretentions to youth wear suspended in front from a string round the loins, a row of from three to twelve shell-shaped embossed plates of bell-metal, from three to six inches in diameter, the largest in the middle and diminishing in size toward the hip; these plates rattle and clink as they move, like prisoner's chains. Very young girls, except for warmth, wear nothing but these appendages; the smallest are never seen without them, and even adult females often have no other covering. The hill Mirees are closely allied to the Abors, the Mirees of the plains being an off-shoot. There are other clans that crop their hair like the Abors, and all are of the same Mongolian type of features.

Many of the Mirees of the plains have become

disciples of an Assamese "Gohain," but they never are so far Hinduized as to give up eating pork beef, and fowls, and drinking liquor.

They join in Assamese festivals, especially the "Behu," and come in groups to the station, men with drums and cymbals, and girls to accompany the music with dancing, gathering money by their performances.

Their houses are built on piles, and their pigs and poultry herd underneath. The hill Mirees are muscular men; they gather their hair in a knot on the forehead, and bind a band of brass knobs around the head.

The Chiefs wear in their ears a silver ornament, the size and shape of a wine glass, and a cane cap with a peak behind, over which is a huge tiger or leopard skin, including the tail, giving them a droll appearance. Their nether garment is a scarf fastened in a girdle of cane, and over the shoulders, a half cape made of fibres of the palm-tree. The men are chiefly occupied in journeys to the plains with loads of "manjit;" in trapping animals of all kinds, from an elephant to a mouse, as all is food that comes to their net: the flesh of a tiger is prized as fit food for men, giving them courage and strength, but not suited to *women*.

The women's costume is peculiar: a short petticoat is secured by a broad leathern belt, ornamented with brass bosses; outside this they wear a singular crinoline of cane work; the upper garment is a band of plaited cane work girding the body close under the arms, from this a fragment of cloth depends and covers the breast. They wear bracelets of silver or copper, and anklets of cane; their hair is neatly adjusted parted it in the centre, and allowed it to hang in two braids; their ears are ornamented in an indescribable manner, and on their necks are enormous quantities of turquoise, agate, cornelian, and onyx beads. The Miree women make faithful and obedient wives, and express astonishment at the unbridled tongues of the Assamese women. It is a singular fact that they never weave their own garments, but depend entirely on other tribes for their clothing. Their religion consists in sacrifice to sylvan spirits, and they practice divination from the examination of the entrails of birds. They have some ideas about God and a future world of happiness or misery.

The Aka-Mirees are at the north-west of this tribe; the manner they tattoo their faces, gives them their name. They are a peaceable tribe, and never take up arms uuless under provocation, and then only in open warfare, not in secret attack as is the case with most of the hill tribes.

The Daphlas are a shorter race than the Mirees, but of the same Mongolian type; their villages are large, and they are rich in flocks and herds. Two hundred and thirty-eight *gams* or chiefs are in receipt of black mail from Government to the amount of Rs. 2,543.

They have frequently obliged the Government to send expeditions into their hills on account of lawless raids in British territory; the last which occurred in 1875, seems to have quieted the country. They acknowledge God, but worship only spirits in sacrifice. Polygamy and polyandry exists among them.

Strange stories are told of the savages occupying the hills between the Daphla country and Thibet; they are said to go absolutely naked, and assert that they have an *abhorrence of the smell of clothes!*

The Migees are a small tribe on the northern hills, a set of lawless savages, who levy black mail on any village they choose to prey upon.

MISSIONS.

CHAPTER XX.

THE American Baptists, we suppose, were the first to enter the province for Mission work, subsequent to British occupation.

The first missionaries were Rev. N. Brown and O. T. Cutter,—printers, who came by invitation from Captain Jenkins, Commissioner of Assam, from the Mission in Burmah to Assam. Their original object was to labor among the Shans, and for this purpose they settled first in Sadiya, in 1837. The dialect of the Shans was supposed to differ so little from Burmese, that they expected they still could make useful the language they had already acquired, and it was hoped the work would extend into northern Burmah and China.

At Sadiya they set up the first printing press in Assam, which had been presented by Captain Jenkins to the Mission.

Dr. Judson, the pioneer of Baptist Missions in the East, thus gave expression to his enthusiastic interest in this new effort, "My heart leaps for joy, and swells with gratitude and praise to God, when I think of brother Jones at Bankok, in the southern extremity of the continent, and brother Brown at

Sadiya, in Assam, on the confines of China, and intervening between these distant points, the missions at Ava, Rangoon, Moulmain, Tavoy, Mergui, and all the churches and schools, which are scattered through the Karen wilderness. Happy lot to live in these days! Happy lot to be allowed to bear a part in the glorious work of bringing an apostate world to the feet of Jesus!"

Rev. N. Brown studied the Shan language before leaving Burmah, and compiled a vocabulary of 3,000 words, preparatory to printing the language in the Roman character. Liberal donations were received from Captain Jenkins, Mr. Trevelyan, Mr. C. Bruce, and others.

The missionaries found, however, that Sadiya was not the place to reach the Shans, they were in the midst of Assamese, while the Shan country lay between Assam and Burmah, and the way not being open to reach them, their attention was turned to the Assamese. To do this work more effectively, they removed to Jeypore, and subsequently to Sibsagor, where the Mission has remained up to the present time.

The Press, for many years the *only* one in Assam, issued most of the literature published in the Assamese language; school books, tracts, portions of Scripture, a hymn-book, and a monthly paper, called "the Orunodoi," or dawn of light, were issued from year to year; in 1845 the entire New Testament, translated by Rev. Brown from the Hebrew, was printed, and in 1850, a third edition.

Rev. Brown left Assam on account of ill-health, after more than a score of years of useful labor, but the work of Scripture translation has been carried on, from time to time, by his successors. Rev. M. Whiting issued some of the minor prophets; Dr. Ward translated from the Hebrew, the book of Genesis, part of Exodus, and the Psalms of David. It was the earnest purpose and desire of his heart to complete the translation of the Old Testament, and for this object, after a brief visit to his native land in 1873, he returned to Assam, but was soon called up higher. Lately Rev. A. K. Gurney has issued the books of Joshua and Ruth.

The "Orunodoi," for many years the only paper published in Assam, was widely circulated and read with great interest by natives and others who understood the language; great pains was taken by the early missionaries Brown, Whiting, and Ward to make it attractive and instructive to the people; it was illustrated with engravings by Native Assamese. Its usefulness in diffusing a knowledge of the gospel of Christ, and in imparting information on subjects of scientific and general interest, among an unenlightened people, cannot be estimated ; latterly it had been suffered to decline, and finally closed its long useful career in December 1880. About two years after, the Press establishment was sold to the Assam Tea Co., and removed to Nazerah. There have usually been two Mission bungalows on the tank bund ; the Chapel and Press were on the banks of the Dikho. The church numbers about 200, and the Christian community about twice that number ; a large portion of the church are Coles, emigrants from the Chota Nagpore district, employed on the Tea gardens. Two of their number are employed by the Mission to visit these people at the gardens and hold service with them on the Sabbath ; some of the planters encourage their work, and others oppose it.

Schools for native boys and girls have usually been sustained by the Mission ; and for several years a Boarding School forEurasian children was conducted by Mrs. Ward. At present the resident missionary is Rev. W. E. Witter and wife, recently arrived.

This Mission has two branches in the Naga hills, one at Molong, about two days distant southerly, the other at Kohima, the civil station among the Angami Nagas. At the former station Rev. E. M. Clark and Mrs. C. have lived for some years, without Government protection, among a rude race of savages, learning an unwritten language, isolated from all European society; and in the rainy season shut up in the hills by swollen rivers and malarious paths, a journey to the plains being impracticable. At intervals they can hear from the outside world, by hiring a Naga to go to the nearest Post-office. Often they have been in imminent danger from the blood thirsty habits of the people,—different villages making raids on each other, and cutting off the head and hands of their victims, they carry them off to their village.

Yet even such savages can be affected by the gospel of Christ, a gospel with power to enlighten the darkest mind, and save to the uttermost, and already over twenty have joined the Kingdom of Peace. The Mission has had the services of a most efficient ordained Assamese preacher, who has acquired their language, compiled a large vocabulary, translated portions of scripture and other books, and composed several hymns in their language. This man, Rev. Godhula B. Brown, is now conducting a new station, about a day's journey from Molong, where he has baptised eight Nagas.

Schools are held at each hill station, and taught by Assamese, members of the Sibsagar Church. A girls' school is taught by a *Naga girl.* These schools are aided by a Government grant of Rs. 520. Rev. S. W. Rivenberg has just arrived to join this Mission.

Rev. C. D. King and Mrs. King, missionaries at Kohima, among the Angami Nagas, are favored in being at a civil station, where they are under the protection of British arms, and are not alone; a Magistrate, Surgeon and half a regiment of soldiers with officers are stationed there, and they have telegraphic communication. The Mission work is in its infancy, having begun only one year ago, but there is a prosperous school of Naga youth, who give a willing ear to the gospel message, and attend sabbath services, and show an aptitude for learning.

The Mission work of the American Baptists was commenced in Nowgong in 1841, by Rev. M. Bronson, who labored there many years with good results. He was afterwards joined by Rev. I. J. Stoddard, and Revs. Scott and Dauble: the two latter died of cholera at the station. Subsequently Dr. Bronson removed to the Goahati Mission, and Rev. R. E. Neighbor carried on the work for a few years; Rev. P. H. Moore arrived in January 1880, and is now in charge.

Miss O. Keeler has been for some years an efficient helper in school and Christain work among the native women. This Mission has done a great deal of school work; for several years there has been a large Normal School for boys, and a boarding and day-school for girls.

The labors of the missionaries have been especially directed to the Mikeers, the hill people of the district, and the Normal School at present sustained is intended to train Mikeer and Cacharree youth to teach in schools and preach among their own people. Four Christian women are employed to visit women in their own homes and give religious instruction.

The church numbers 110 and has an ordained native pastor; the station and village schools number thirteen, and the pupils two hundred and thirty-nine, aided by a Government grant of Rs. 1,500.

Tezpore has been a Mission station of the S. P. G. Society for many years, the first missionary, Rev. Mr. Kesselmeyer, has been worthily succeeded by the Rev. Mr. Endle. Their efforts have been chiefly directed to the Cacharree tribe and been fairly successful. A Normal School for training Cacharee youths for teachers and preachers, is held in Tezpore; the schools are aided by a Government grant of Rs. 1,800.

Besides the Tezpore church and schools, there are a number of churches and schools at the Cacharree villages. At "Benghari, a brick church has been built for the Christian worship of the Cacharree converts." English and native worship is also maintained at the church in Tezpore by the Rev. Endle.

At Goahati there is a chaplain appointed by the bishop of Calcutta for Goahati and Shillong, and he divides his time between the two places in holding Sabbath services. There is also a chaplain in Sibsagar and Dibrughur, who occasionally hold service at some of the Tea gardens.

The American Baptists have had a Mission in Goahati for over thirty years. The work was commenced by Rev. Mr. Barker, a tablet to whose worthy memory may be seen in the brick chapel.

He was succeeded by Revs. Danforth, Ward, Comfort, and Bronson. At present the Mission is in charge of an ordained native preacher, Rev. Kandura Smith, who conducts worship on the Sabbath in the chapel and visits the churches in the vicinity. Connected with the Mission are fourteen churches, with six hundred and fourteen members, over one hundred of whom were added last year. A girls' school is held at the Mission, and in the village schools are over two hundred pupils. The most successful mission in the province, is that of the Welsh Calvinistic society among the Khassias ; there are two very good reasons for this result ; the work is among a people free from the trammels of *caste*, and the field has been well supplied with missionaries since it commenced, over thirty years ago, by Rev. W. J. Lewis.

His successful labours have been well followed up by others, till the work has spread over the hills.

Rev. T. J. Jones is now in charge at Shillong, assisted by six other missionaries, stationed at as many different places in the hills: at Mowphong there is a medical mission; at Cherra, a Normal school, and scattered over the hills ninety schools for boys and girls; a larger number of girls are under instruction in this district than in any other in Assam. It is possible among these people to have *mixed* schools, which is impracticable among Hindus or Mahomedans. Connected with the Mission are sixty-six churches, numbering over 2,000 members, and the Christian adherents are over 3,000. The people are characterized as gentle in disposition, truthful and industrious, free from the prejudices of caste, and readily listen to the gospel news of salvation through the Lord Jesus. They were never idolaters, their worship consisting in sacrifices to evil spirits.

The American Baptist Mission for several years held property on the Goalpara hills, the labors of Rev. I. J. Stoddard and his successor, Rev. T. J. Keith, being chiefly among the Garo tribe. An interesting incident was the means of starting the work:

Two men of the tribe who were in police service at Goahati, and stationed at one of the Mission bungalows, where an officer was living, picked up a Christian tract on the premises; they read it, were interested, and sought further instruction, and by the blessing of God, became firm believers. They left Government service, and went to make known the good news of salvation among their own people. The work prospered; both these first converts have been ordained, and, up to the present time, are actively engaged in the good work. Rev. I. J. Stoddard gathered the first harvest from the good seed sown among them, baptising hundreds, and forming them into churches. Schools were opened, and some elementary books issued in the Garo language, but the Bengalee language has been chiefly taught in the schools. Rev. T. J. Keith succeeded Mr. Stoddard, whose health failed; he published a dictionary in Garo, Bengalee and English, and a grammar. He returned to America and was succeeded by Revs. E. G. Phillips and M. Mason who continued to reside in Goalpara, till about 1877 when, in order to be *among* the people, they removed to Tura, a civil station, recently opened on the Garo hills. Goalpara has since been unoccupied as a Mission station.

Considering the brief period this Mission has been in progress, and the very limited amount of labor bestowed, the results promise grand results in the future. The Scriptures are being translated by the present missionaries, Rev. Phillips and Mason, and some of the gospels have been printed; a new dictionary is in preparation, and a monthly sheet issued, called "The Garos' Friend." Nine churches have been formed at different villages, with over eight hundred members, mostly administered to by native preachers, six of whom are ordained.

A girls' Boarding School in Tura is taught by Miss M. Russell; in the villages there are thirty-five schools, numbering six hundred and sixty-two pupils. A Normal school is held in Tura. The Government make a liberal grant of Rs. 3,000 to sustain these schools. The people also contribute liberally from their scanty means in aid of Christian work.

The Garo tribe, number about 109,000, and it is evident the work among them is really only begun.

If we consider what these people have been in the past,—nearly naked savages, filthy, and barbarous in their habits and customs,—and observe the change Christianity has wrought, we shall be constrained to praise the God of Missions.

Any one desiring tangible proof of the good that has been accomplished, can visit one of the Christian villages, and look upon a company of these once naked, ignorant heathen, neatly clothed, and assembled for the worship of the one true and living God. No foreign teacher is present; one of their own number spreads before them the treasures of God's word; you may hear them sing the praises of

God in their own strange tongue, but in tunes familiar to your childhood's ear heard under the frescoed domes of your fatherland ; then all devoutly kneeling, the voice of prayer ascends to the unseen God. Can you then ask doubtfully whether Missions are a success or failure ?

Our limited view of the country and its people will not admit of any extended description of the Hindu religion ; a *full* description of the hoary system of idolatry, which most of the people follow, fills two large quarto volumes of about five hundred pages each, of "Ward's View of Hinduism," and is the subject of many volumes by other authors.

A glimpse of the manner in which Hinduism controls the social and private life of the people even to their minutest concerns, in a measure, is scattered through the foregoing pages. The great annual festivals, "Behu," "Roth Jatra," "Durgapuja" and "Dhewali" are apparently great holidays, especially for the children, but the rigid Hindu has many days of sacred observance ; but these bring only a few of the most devout to the temple for worship. The temples everywhere are decaying, fit emblems of the system they represent. The breath of heaven scatters the seeds of trees into the crevices of these structures, where by germinating and enlarging their shoots gradually, the stones are loosened and fall

In like manner heaven is sowing the seeds of divine truth, through civilization and Christianity, that are germinating in every part of this vast structure of heathenism, and though now, only here and there, a living stone falls out and is transferred to the temple of the true God, the whole must inevitably be destroyed. This result is anticipated even by its present strong adherents, and often expressed. The aged and grey-haired will cling to the *debris* of their wrecked dependence, till the waves of death roll over them, but this will set free their sons and daughters from the restraints that now bind them to a system in which they have lost faith, and open the way for them to express their acceptance of the truth as it is in Christ Jesus.

FINIS.